"In twenty-five y[...] [...]n lives become di[...] [...]n, loss, or some oth[...] [...]g is that some people emerge on the other end of suffering having been somehow enlarged by it. How does that happen? What goes on in the brain, the mind, the heart, or the soul to bring one more fully into life? What can we do beyond leaving it to chance or hoping that we will be enlivened?

"In *Meant-to-Be Moments,* Mary Treacy O'Keefe explores these mysteries in the best possible way—through stories. And she goes further—she offers a method that we can use with our own stories to encounter God and our own deepest selves within the stuff of our lives."

—Henry Emmons, MD, PhD
Author of *The Chemistry of Joy* and *The Chemistry of Calm*

"As a spiritual director, I'm thrilled to have discovered this compelling and well-written book. Often when people come to see me it is because they are dealing with life-and-death issues, or those surrounding grief. I'm delighted to have *Meant-to-Be Moments* in my cache of helpful tools. Filled with wonderful first person accounts, it is a book I can wholeheartedly recommend because it enlightens, educates, and entertains in such a delightful and uplifting way."

—Diane Keyes, spiritual director
Award-winning author of *This Sold House* and *Spirit of the Snowpeople*

"*Meant-to-Be Moments* is an invitation and a call to wake up and pay attention to the grace and mystery that surround us. What makes the stories extraordinary is the fact that they are very ordinary—happening to people in the course of their everyday lives. Invariably, the gift that emerges in the stories is clarity and serenity. Through observing signs, experiencing synchronicities, and reflecting, people discover purpose and meaning, and life makes more sense. Mary Treacy O'Keefe offers profound spiritual wisdom that transcends cultures and traditions. It offers inspiration and hope."

—Mary Jo Kreitzer, PhD, RN,
FAAN Director, Center for Spirituality & Healing;
Professor, School of Nursing, University of Minnesota

"First, a tear alert. Have your box of tissues handy. Mary Treacy O'Keefe has gathered nearly sixty stories as told to her by people who have had 'meant-to-be' happenings. This compilation of stories demonstrates how spiritual transformation can give people the courage to live life fully and be who they are meant-to-be. These stories affirm that God is an active force in our daily lives—if we pay attention, listen, and respond to that small, still voice we hear. *Meant-to-Be Moments* present themselves in a variety of ways—as signs, dreams, telepathic events, and synchronicity. These encourage you to make time to care for others as well as yourself. Need a spiritual kick in the pants? This book is for you."

—Connie Anderson, author of *When Polio Came Home:
How Ordinary People Overcame Extraordinary Challenges*
and *In My Next Life I Want to be My Dog*

"My favorite storytellers now have some serious competition from Mary Treacy O'Keefe. I love listening to and learning from stories, and the stories in *Meant-to-Be Moments* are packed with joy, pathos, love, coincidence, compassion, and a heartfelt connection with the divine.

"These stories help us to accept that human part of us that rages and wrestles with illness, dying, and death. At the same time, they inspire us to embrace our higher selves as we discover our deep spiritual connection with friends, family, and God.

"As I smiled and cried my way through the book, I realized how deeply touched I was by this emotionally rich and profound collection of stories. Thank you, Mary, for this delightful and amazing gift."

—Bill Manahan, MD
Past president, American Holistic Medical Association

"We've all experienced those moments of coincidence, those serendipitous events that seem pleasantly strange at the time they happen. *Meant-to-Be Moments* provides a beautiful combination of teaching us how to tap into these moments with more intention while interweaving real-life stories of ordinary people experiencing extraordinary moments of 'coincidence.' If you have ever wondered if 'things happen for a reason,' then you need to read Mary Treacy O'Keefe's book. She is the perfect guide to help you answer that question for yourself."

—Pamela Muldoon
Producer/host, Next Stage Online Radio

"*Meant-to-Be Moments* is inspiring, insightful, and comforting. It is profoundly spiritual but universal in its understanding of God. *Meant-to-Be Moments* sharpens the reader's awareness of the many 'thin places' that take place in daily life. These occurrences often go unnoticed, written off as hunches, accidents, coincidences, or they are simply forgotten. In reading the book I found myself remembering a number of situations that could have been helpful to me had I given them my full attention. I started to read this manuscript with the intention of quickly skimming it. I found myself hungrily reading every word and taking long pauses to digest what I had just read.

"Mary Treacy O'Keefe has given the world a great gift. This book is a must-read for therapists, hospice workers, medical personnel, and clergy."

—Jeanne M. Wiger, PhD
Marriage and family therapist

Meant-to-Be Moments:

Discovering What We are Called to Do and Be

Meant-To-Be Moments

Discovering What We Are Called to Do and Be

MARY TREACY O'KEEFE

ISBN 13: 978-1-940014-33-3
eISBN 13: 978-1-940014-34-0
Library of Congress Number: 2014948556
Printed in the United States of America

18 17 16 15 14   5 4 3 2 1

Author Headshot photo: Dani Werner of Daniphoto
Cover photo: Mary Treacy O'Keefe

Scripture quotations marked NASB are taken from the New American Standard Bible®,
Copyright © 1960, 1962, 1963, 1968, 1971, 1972, 1973, 1975, 1977, 1995 by
The Lockman Foundation. Used by permission. (www.Lockman.org)

Scripture quotations marked NIV are taken from the Holy Bible, New International
Version ®, NIV ®, copyright © 1973, 1978, 1984, 2011 by Biblica, Inc. TM.
Used by permission of Zondervan. All rights reserved worldwide.

Book Design by Ryan Scheife / Mayfly Design
Typeset in the Whitman and Worcester typefaces

Published by Wise Ink Creative Publishing
Minneapolis, Minnesota
www.wiseinkpub.com

To order, visit www.itascabooks.com or call 1-800-901-3480.
Reseller discounts available.

With love and gratitude, this book is dedicated to
Dan, Peter, Bill, Emily, and Tim

Contents

Finding Meaning in Meant-to-be Moments

"*Get out of the car,*" a voice inside me whispered one cold Minnesota evening as my boyfriend and I sat talking in his car in front of my parents' home. Not wanting to explain to Dan (now my husband of more than forty years) that I was hearing voices, I ignored it. But when that voice became an urgent command, "Get out of the car, NOW!" I obeyed. Moments after my perplexed date and I were safely inside the house, a drunk driver smashed into Dan's car and sent it careening into the neighbor's yard.

There was an explanation for the accident: the driver drank too much, lost control of his car, and drove head-long into ours. Yet the voice I heard seemed meant to be: It saved our lives. *But where had the voice come from?* Had it been luck? My overactive imagination? Or was it the "still, small voice" that Scripture says comes from God? (1 Kings 19:12 KJV)

SINCE THAT LONG-AGO INCIDENT AND OTHERS LIKE IT, I'VE wondered: *Are some experiences meant to be? Does God really call us to be a certain way and do certain things? Is there really a Divine master plan? And if so, what is our role in that plan?*

To know why things happen, to know whether a higher power has a grand plan for us, to know what our true purpose in life may be—these are the philosophical and spiritual questions humans have pondered for centuries. Now more than ever, we want to know the answers.

People of all cultures and faiths are in the midst of the most intense renewal of interest in spirituality and religion since the late 1800s. Influential philosopher and psychologist William James's definition of religion, as described in *The Varieties of Religious Experience,* is as true today as it was more than one hundred years ago when he wrote that human beings are incurably religious. He defined religion not as particular theological doctrines but rather as "the feelings, acts, or experiences that help one understand whatever one considers divine."

For many people, this is the essence of religion in modern day America. The quest for spiritual growth, regardless of religious belief, is especially prevalent among Americans. As nests empty, parents die, and retirement looms, baby boomers, in particular, are seeking a sense of purpose. And the percentage of those searching for spiritual growth continues to rise, from six in ten people in the early 1990s to eight in ten in 2001, according to George Gallup, Jr. In his article, *Americans Feel a Need to Believe,* he concluded:

Even as scientists continue to advance human-kind's knowledge about everything from the age of the universe to the protein sequence in a DNA strand, Gallup polls indicate that Americans' need to believe in matters beyond mortal ken is greater than ever.

I belong among the soul-searchers. In the many years since my near-miss in that parked car, I've come to believe that the voice I heard was from a sacred source, possibly an angelic messenger, perhaps the guardian angel my mother insisted protected each of her ten children. On that night a Divine voice spoke directly to me for the first time—or, at least, for the first time I was listening—and I knew in that moment that God not only exists, but cares about me.

Although I still don't know how it happened or why we were spared, I have no doubt God communicates with all of us through a "still, small voice," much like the one I heard on that wintry night so long ago. Sacred scripture affirms that belief:

And he said, Go forth, and stand upon the mount before the Lord. And, behold, the Lord passed by, and a great and strong wind rent the mountains, and broke in pieces the rocks before the Lord; but the Lord was not in the wind; and after the wind an earthquake, but the Lord was not in the earthquake. And after the earthquake a fire, but the Lord was not in the fire, and after the fire a still, small voice. (1 Kings 19: 11–12, KJV)

I don't believe God causes car accidents, earthquakes, or fires. I don't believe God is responsible for the deadly consequences that may follow when people misuse the gift of freedom of choice. But I do believe God can be found *within* tragic events if we listen for that still, small voice and pay attention to the countless ways God's love is manifested. Meant-to-be moments are tangible ways by which God invites us to *be* guided, comforted, and awed during the best, worst, and everyday moments of our lives. Meant-to-be moments also motivate us to *do* things that enable us to be the person we are called to be.

That God can be found within tragedy was never clearer to me than when my parents died within three months of each other. It was then that I felt the unmistakable presence of a higher power in my daily life through a series of events known as "thin places." There are many ways to experience God's presence in our lives, regardless of religious belief. Soul friendships, centering prayer, Scripture, nature, religious rituals, personal prayer, and discernment all reinforce our unique relationship with God. But it was our thin-place experiences—momentary connections between this world and the next in which we behold the Divine—that comforted my siblings and me as we mourned our parents. Each connection seemed to happen for a reason. Each moment during that sad but sacred time seemed "meant to be," the phrase we often used to describe them. When we understand a meant-to-be experience as being Divinely orchestrated, it also can be called a "thin place."

Meant-to-be Moments

Thin places fall into the broader category of spiritual experiences I call meant-to-be moments. Meant-to-be moments appear in many forms: as signs or messages, such as rainbows after a loved one dies (as was the case with my parents) or in the return of a long-lost item. Sometimes meant-to-be moments materialize as dreams that give us a second chance to say goodbye to a loved one who died suddenly, or as premonitions, such as the one that stops us from boarding an elevator that moments later gets stuck, or urges us to exit a parked car that is about to be hit. Maybe the meant-to-be moment is a chance meeting or a narrow escape. Maybe it's a nagging feeling that steers us away from trouble or toward a fortuitous opportunity.

Some meant-to-be moments seem positively miraculous, such as the appearance of angels and visions of deceased loved ones. Other meant-to-be moments are subtle, like the flash of insight that provides an answer to a seemingly impossible dilemma at work. Whether the event rescues us from danger, eases a passing anxiety, or answers a troubling question, it becomes a meant-to-be moment when it is too serendipitous to be accidental, too significant to be random.

Why is it that we seek meaning, even during the most tragic events? During my radio interview with bestselling author Dr. Joan Borysenko a few years ago, she described a flight she took not long after Sept. 11, 2001. She noticed several passengers reading *Man's Search for Meaning*, Victor

Frankl's chronicle of his years as a Holocaust prisoner. *Were they searching for ways in which to understand the horrific events of 9/11? How could the death and destruction of that day have happened for any other reason than to manifest the evil intentions of those who caused it?* Even when such questions are unanswerable, reflecting on them helps us give our own meaning to difficult times.

In his foreword to a later edition of Frankl's *Man's Search for Meaning,* Rabbi Harold Kushner wrote, "Suffering in and of itself is meaningless; we give our suffering meaning by the way in which we respond to it." Both Frankl and Kushner agree that we cannot always control what happens to us in our lives, but we can control how we respond to what happens to us.

Ultimately, Frankl believed the greatest task for any person is to find meaning in his or her life. Meant-to-be moments help us to discover our purpose—who we are meant to be and what we are meant to do.

A Formula for Living Fully

Whether they occur in the presence or absence of faith, meant-to-be moments can lead to profound spiritual awakenings. Whether they happen in good times or bad, they help us make connections, not only to the past, but also to opportunities in the present and future. Meant-to-be moments have the power to inspire, motivate, and heal. They also have the power to transform.

Bearing witness to personal and spiritual transformation gives others the courage to do the same. Since I wrote about my family's meant-to-be experiences in my first book, *Thin Places: Where Faith Is Affirmed and Hope Dwells*, hundreds of believers and nonbelievers alike have eagerly shared their own meant-to-be stories with me.

These stories have been a source of endless inspiration and joy to me. They have affirmed my faith and my belief that God is an active force in our daily lives, if only we learn to pay attention, discern meaning, and respond. In my role as a spiritual director, the co-founder of the holistic center known as Well Within, and the host of WebTalkRadio's "Hope, Healing, and WellBeing" show, I have witnessed others transformed by the realization of the Divine in their daily lives.

These stories of transformation are the heart of *Meant-to-be Moments*. The book's soul is a four-step process, a practical formula for living a more intentional life by paying attention, discerning, and responding to our meant-to-be moments. Each story illuminates one or more steps in my Living Fully formula:

Pay Attention: Mind the Meant-to-be Moments

Reflect: What am I Called to Do and Be?

Ask and Acknowledge: Deepening Our Relationship with God

Say Yes! Responding to Meant-to-be Moments

Step 1 of the Living Fully process urges us to Pay Attention or "mind" the meant-be-moments in our lives. Meant-to-be moments present themselves in various ways:

synchronicities or coincidences that transcend the ordinary; as Divine communication in the form of thin-place moments; and as the spiritual experiences of people with belief systems different from our own. Sometimes, as with my experience in the car, we are also called to "mind"—or "obey"—a meant-to-be directive without having time to reflect upon its meaning.

Step 2 invites us to Reflect on what we are called to do or be by finding meaning within meant-to-be moments. Thoughtful, prayerful questions help us make sense of our life experiences. Testing our experience against scripture, reason, and wise counsel from spiritual mentors helps us discern God's will for us. Reflecting on how meant-to-be moments will strengthen our relationships with others, with ourselves, and with the Divine helps us decide how to respond to them. As we become more aware of Divine Providence, as manifested in meant-to-be moments, our relationship with God deepens.

Step 3 encourages us to Ask and Acknowledge by requesting assurance and help and by being grateful to Divine Providence when our prayers are answered or when we observe a meant-to-be moment. This step encourages us to ask for comfort in times of grief and wisdom to make the right choices for our lives. It demonstrates the importance of asking for and acknowledging the clarity and guidance that leads to a relationship with God based on mutual trust and love.

Step 4 prompts us to Say Yes! and respond to meant-to-be moments by taking good care of ourselves and being a channel of love to others.

These four steps enable our meant-to-be moments to guide us toward a life of purpose and meaning, whereby we love ourselves, others, and our God more deeply. In doing so, we are fulfilling God's most important commandment: to "*love the Lord your God with all your heart and with all your soul and with all your strength and with all your mind and love your neighbor as yourself.*" Luke 10:27 (NIV)

Socrates said, "An unexamined life is not worth living." Our search for meaning—to know why things happen, to know whether a higher power has a grand plan for us—requires discernment. Discernment fuels our personal and spiritual growth. That growth prepares us to receive the gifts of comfort, healing, inspiration, forgiveness, and grace. Ultimately, as we share these gifts with others, our true purpose is at last revealed:

We know *who* we are meant to be.

We are living fully.

We are living intentionally.

We know *what* we are meant to do.

STEP I

Pay Attention:
Mind the Meant-to-be Moments

STEP 1 OF THE LIVING FULLY PROCESS ENCOURAGES US TO Pay Attention to our meant-to-be experiences. There are innumerable types, including nature's transcendent beauty, significant coincidences, the "still, small voice" that provides guidance when we most need it, and the people who show up in our lives to teach us about beliefs that differ from our own.

CHAPTER 1

Pay Attention to Meant-to-be Moments

COINCIDENCES ARE ONE OF THE MOST COMMON TYPES OF meant-to-be moments. As the adage says, "Coincidences are God's way of remaining anonymous." Many people say, "there's no such thing as coincidences," believing that they are a powerful way to experience providence. The stories below come from people who share that belief:

> Ruth's room was located near the kitchen in the back wing of the hospice facility. My shifts varied, but I had looked in on her often, for about a month, to see if there was anything she needed to make her more comfortable. She never had visitors on my rounds, and I learned she had been eating poorly for weeks. She was pale, quiet, and calm; I knew she was getting ready to leave this earth. I'd often fluff her pillow, moisten her lips, or simply sit with her, holding her hand while listening to her irregular breathing.

A few weeks later, I reluctantly left my hospice work when we'd finished the relocation of our home and business to another city three hundred miles away. I often wondered when Ruth, and the other patients I'd cared for, had passed. I believed working in the residential hospice facility was a privilege—like being a midwife on the other end of life as souls transitioned to the next phase of existence. Always a mystical and profoundly beautiful experience, it was an honor to be present when death came.

After settling in and getting life up and running in our new home, I set up a small counseling practice and joined the local hospice, although it was not a residential care facility. I became involved with bereavement groups and was delighted when their plans for an expanded center became a reality. I happily volunteered to help with decor and furnishing decisions.

I often relied upon a young man in a local furniture store to help me make selections for my home and solve decorating problems. So I went by his store one day to see if he could help with the items the hospice needed while keeping to a tight budget. A young woman named Suzanne approached me and said it was Dan's day off, but she'd be happy to help me, giving him the credit from any purchases. I explained I was buying for the new local hospice center.

She brightened and said her mom had such wonderful hospice care before she died. She was so grateful for the attention given to her mother since Suzanne couldn't get up to see her as often as she liked due to her work schedule. I asked where her mom had died, and she said "Seattle." I told her I had worked in a care facility in Seattle a few years earlier and wondered if it was the same one. It was. She said she had always wanted to thank the person who cared for her mother in the final days of her life. I asked her mother's name, and she said it was "Ruth." Her mother had told her about a woman who sat with her often and respected her desires for peace and quiet, and how much she appreciated her presence.

I told her I was that woman. Suzanne couldn't believe it. She said she had prayed to be able to talk with the person who walked with her mom in the last days of her life. We shared hugs and tears. After years and miles apart, Suzanne got to thank her mother's caretaker.

Had Dan been in the store that day, we would not have met. Some things are meant to be.

—MARLENE KING

Meant-to-be moments, such as Marlene's story, transcend the ordinary realm of intuition and coincidence. They are, in fact, too extraordinary to be ignored, too significant to be random. Meant-to-be moments present themselves in a variety of ways—as signs, dreams, telepathic events, and synchronicities—often coming from a variety of cultures, traditions, and beliefs. The more attentive we are to such moments, the more aware we become of just how often they occur. And the more attentive we are, the closer we come to discovering our greater purpose.

Synchronicity best describes Marlene's meant-to-be experience. Carl Jung described synchronicity as the "meaningful coincidence of two or more events, where something other than the probability of chance is involved. If one is impressed by such things, one could call it (synchronicity) a minor miracle."

That Marlene and Suzanne should meet was coincidence enough. But what are the chances that so many coincidences would be at play to make their connection possible? That Marlene should be in the store on a day that Suzanne was working? That they would discuss hospice, that Suzanne's mother had told her about Marlene, and that Marlene should have moved to a city where Suzanne lived? As Marlene says, meeting her former patient's daughter seemed truly meant to be. And for Suzanne, the experience enabled her to *be* grateful to both Marlene and to the God who answered her prayers.

Coincidences Bring Comfort

Some of the most dramatic meant-to-be moments occur during the time surrounding the death of a loved one.

Charlene's family found comfort in the synchronicities that seemed to explain a prophetic vision her daughter-in-law had a few days before she died:

> Our daughter-in-law, Heidi, died from melanoma on June 24, 2012. It was her thirty-eighth birthday, and she died exactly nine months after her diagnosis. Sometime during the last week of her life, she was lying on the bed, having a conversation with our son, her husband, Mitchell. During the conversation she suddenly closed her eyes and drifted away, saying softly, "Hi guys." Then she opened her eyes and came back to reality. When our son asked her what had just happened, she replied, "I was just saying 'hi' to everyone who was around me in my boat."
>
> On the morning of her birthday, Heidi's cousin read something to her from the book *PRAYERS FOR HEALING: 365 Blessings, Poems, and Meditations From Around The World*. The reading for June 24 was written by Saint John of the Cross who was born in 1542:

> And I saw the river
> over which every soul must pass
> to reach the kingdom of heaven
> and the name of that river was suffering
> And I saw the boat
> which carries souls across the river
> and the name of that boat was love.

Heidi's cousin did not know about Heidi's previous conversation with Mitchell until later.

—CHARLENE RHODES

Charlene and her family have always believed in the afterlife. As she says, "This incident affirmed that there is so much more to come." Heidi was a pastor, having been ordained four months before her diagnosis. She loved her pastoring and was a pastor till the day she died. Heidi's story is a thin-place affirmation of the faith she so passionately shared with others; it enabled her family to *be* reassured that there must be something wondrous beyond this earthly realm.

Synchronicity is at the heart of the next story as well, in which a best friend and grieving mother experience a similar sign from a young man who had committed suicide.

Three Signs Comfort a Grieving Mother and Best Friend

I can't imagine a greater loss than the death of one's child. Within our circle of close friends, a couple of families have lost their beloved young adult sons and my heart breaks for them and any other parent who has lost a son or daughter. This story is about an event that occurred after the death of Mark, the best friend of our own son, Bill. Our sadness for Mark's family was compounded by our son's grief at losing his closest friend since the boys first met in the fourth grade. We learned of Mark's death when his aunt called to say he had committed suicide the previous night. Their family knew Bill would be devastated, so she wanted him to learn of this tragedy directly from us.

Everyone who knew Mark was shocked to hear of his death. All his life, he was one of those people who lit up a room when he entered. Even as a child, he had an amazing ability to banter and exhibit his sharp wit with people of all ages. Bill and Mark shared a passion for baseball. So his parents and I spent many weekend afternoons watching our sons play ball, with my husband, Dan, as the team's coach. Mark's love of sports propelled him toward a career in sports broadcasting. He attained his goal when he was hired as a radio announcer in a small town in Montana.

After Mark had left his Minnesota home, Bill kept in touch with him via weekly phone calls. Bill worried about his friend living so far from his close-knit family and his many friends. He knew Mark would miss the parties that inevitably welcomed him whenever he was in Minnesota. Mark enjoyed his liquor, especially one particular brand of Vodka. He encouraged others to try his favorite drink, often adding, "You've got to try this stuff. It's so smooth." With his outgoing, fun personality, Mark never gave any indication to his family or friends that he intended to end his own life.

Immediately after hearing about Mark's tragic death, Dan and I called Bill at work and told him to come home. After sharing the news of his friend's death, we all sobbed. Mark was like a fourth son to Dan and me. When he visited our home, he never bothered to knock at the front door, knowing he was welcome anytime. Our hearts ached for

Bill and for Mark's family. On that first night of tear-filled grief, I asked God to send a sign to comfort all of us.

The next day, Bill felt a strong need to be with Mark's family so he could mourn this loss together with his own second family. As he stepped inside Mark's home, he was engulfed with hugs. Mark's parents later told us that Bill was the perfect person to show up at the worst time of their lives. Together, they not only shed many tears, but also laughed together; it was impossible not to, after Bill told them stories of Mark's antics they had never heard before.

As Bill drove home, he said he saw the first of three signs that would eventually provide solace for himself, Mark's family, and us. Driving along a four-lane highway, a mile or so from our house, he noticed a white paneled delivery truck as it passed by him. Upon observing the painted logo on the side of the truck, he gasped. It was a picture of Mark's favorite brand of vodka. Underneath the bottle was a tag line, the exact words Mark often used to describe the product: "It's so smooth." Bill's instant thought was that Mark was trying to communicate a message to him via a sign he knew would make sense to his best friend.

When Bill arrived home, he told me what he'd just seen. I agreed it might be a sign from Mark, but I also asked Bill about his own interpretation of the incident.

"It's like he's trying to tell me something, maybe that it was the vodka that caused him to commit suicide." Bill paused before continuing, as if he'd already thought about possible reasons for why he had seen the van. "And maybe Mark's also trying to tell me to *be* careful about my own drinking habits."

As if to reaffirm the significance of the sign, the identical truck appeared again two days later when Bill was driving home from the cemetery following Mark's burial. He said it was "kind of weird to see this truck twice in a row" when he'd never noticed it before. Bill knows I believe that when things happen in threes, they often are "meant-to-be" signs. To me, it's like God is telling us to pay special attention to whatever occurred. So my son wasn't surprised when I suggested he especially be alert because he probably would see the truck again soon.

But it wasn't Bill who noticed the truck the third time. It was Mark's mother, Anne, who saw it, the day after she buried her son. I learned this when I stopped by her house that afternoon. As we visited about the funeral and discussed how she was coping, I mentally wondered if she had noticed anything that seemed like a sign from Mark but didn't want to ask her. As if to respond to my unexpressed inquiry, she told me about an experience she'd had that morning.

She began, "Maybe I was just searching for any sort of sign from Mark," she paused, then continued, "but this morning, I saw this white truck with a vodka bottle on the side of it." Anne didn't mention noticing the tag line but noticed something else: on the driver's side door were printed the words "Johnson Brothers Distributors," the same last name as her own family.

"What did seeing the truck mean to you?" I asked Anne.

"I feel like Mark is trying to tell me something" she responded.

"What do you think he is trying to say?"

"I think he wants me to know that his drinking problem might have caused him to take his own life."

I gently asked how that interpretation made her feel. She said, "It comforts me greatly to have some sort of explanation for this tragedy. I feel like his spirit is still with me and our family and that brings me peace."

I hadn't planned on telling her about Bill's similar experience, as I was unsure if it would upset her. But after hearing about Anne's reaction to seeing the truck, I told her it was the third time that a similar truck had appeared after Mark's death. Like me, Anne also felt like "things in threes are meant to be."

Anne and her husband, Mike, have had other experiences of Mark's continuing presence in their lives, like when she heard an inner whisper saying, "I'm so sorry" and "I love you." Although Mark's family always will grieve for their beloved son, these signs from God—and Mark—have reassured them that the love that they all have for each other will never die. These meant-to-be moments have enabled their family—and ours—to *be* comforted and to *be* at peace, even in the midst of our grief.

———————

FOR MANY PEOPLE, SYNCHRONOUS MEANT-TO-BE MOMENTS follow a numerical pattern. For example, the number three is considered by some to be a sign of the Divine in Celtic and Native American traditions, among others. When a similar incident happens three times, it may be time to pay attention to what it means.

I mentioned this point during a talk at a conference for

cancer survivors several years ago. Afterward, a woman in the audience shared with me her own story of things happening in threes.

Triple "Bashert" Experiences

While vacationing in the Bahamas, Dale often took long walks along the beach near the resort where she was staying. One afternoon she met another woman, Debby, doing the same. They introduced themselves, and then walked together, chatting nonstop. Dale learned that Debby was in the midst of a weeklong cruise that included just a few hours on this particular island. The pair bonded instantly, experiencing that immediate connection that so often precedes a good friendship.

Before returning to her cruise ship, Debby introduced Dale to her traveling companion who had decided to read and sunbathe on the beach rather than walk. Debby and her friend spent the remaining two hours of their shore excursion visiting with Dale. During their discussion of a variety of topics, including families, careers, and books, synchronicity revealed itself: All three were Jewish women married to Christian men and each had two children. And each woman was reading the same book, *The Red Tent*.

Though Dale was from Minnesota and the other two women were from Los Angeles, they felt that they had known each other forever. By the end of their brief visit, they had exchanged email addresses and vowed to stay in touch.

One week after returning home, Dale was diagnosed with breast cancer. When she emailed her new friends with the news, she learned that Debby's mom had had breast cancer so her daughter participated in several Avon Walks for Breast Cancer. During Dale's treatment, both of her new friends were supportive. Their response to her challenging situation—when Dale needed it most—helped strengthen the bonds of their new friendship. Although this incident occurred many years ago, Dale and Debby remain in touch and occasionally travel to visit in person with each other.

The three women who learned how much they had in common during three short hours together all believe that the synchronicities that enabled them to *be* good friends makes it *bashert*—a Yiddish word that describes the Jewish concept of meant to be.

———————

SOMETIMES IT'S NOT EXTRAORDINARY COINCIDENCE BUT *intuition* that signifies a meant-to-be moment. Call it a hunch or sixth sense but we've all experienced it—times when we just *know* something is so, without proof or prior knowledge. For example, isn't that feeling you are forgetting something always accurate? It is for me! I also witnessed the power of intuition in generating innovative ideas for products and strategies when I was marketing manager. I worked for a firm that facilitates creative process sessions for Fortune 500 companies. Intuition is a gift cherished by some of the world's most impressive business executives.

In his inspiring book, *Be My Guest*, hotel magnate Conrad Hilton attributed much of his professional success to his intuition, or "hunch decision-making." Interestingly,

Hilton's four-step decision-making process included a spiritual dimension. First, he *sat quietly* in an empty Roman Catholic cathedral. Next, he *visualized* the problem or opportunity facing him. Then he *listened* for the answer, and finally he *acted* on it. More often than not, his process worked.

Telepathy IS YET ANOTHER WAY TO REACH OUT TO A FRIEND or family member. Telepathy, which literally means "distant experience," is extrasensory communication via thoughts, ideas, feelings, and imagery. It is recognized as an ability within certain tribal cultures, including Australian aborigines, and as a gift among mystics and psychics.

In fact, we all possess telepathic ability. Have you ever answered a ringing phone, only to hear the familiar voice of someone you were just thinking about? And what about the times you prayed for guidance or help, then someone reached out to you as if in direct response to your request? Jung's concept of synchronicity includes telepathic communication: moments when we experience similar or identical thoughts at the same time but in different places.

The following stories illustrate how people from a distance perceived that another person needed help.

Sensing a Need to Reach Out

One busy Saturday morning, Robin felt she should call an old friend, the wife of one of her husband's medical school classmates. Both men became surgeons and their families remained close despite living hundreds of miles apart.

Robin is a compassionate and caring person, but she put off the call for a while, distracted by the demands of driving her children to school and sports activities. Yet she could not get thoughts of her friend out of her mind, so she took the time to call.

When the friend, Sandy, picked up the phone and heard Robin's voice, she began to cry. The woman's husband, Tom, had just found out that he had an advanced stage of cancer. Shocked and terrified, the couple had not told anyone about the diagnosis, and they were unsure how his family and their own young children should be told. Robin's call came when her friend desperately needed to talk with someone, as if Robin had somehow heard her friend's silent plea for help.

Robin's husband also responded with compassion to this sad situation by traveling out-of-state to perform surgeries when Tom was too sick to do so himself.

Over time, Robin has learned to trust her intuitive promptings. No matter how busy she is, she makes the time to contact people she is concerned about. She feels God is calling her to *do* something by helping others, and she is happy to respond.

A Distant Prayer

Cheryl was hundreds of miles away from her grandson when she not only sensed but saw, in a vision, that he was dangerously ill. Her response indicates one of the best things we can *do* when anxious about another person: to offer prayers for his or her protection:

On the way to get my daypack from the tent, I stop, my leg muscles refusing to propel me forward. I am barely aware of the lapping of the waves on the shore and shifting patterns of sunlight filtering through the tall red pines. These common sounds and sights of Canada's Quetico Provincial Park fade to a backdrop. My mind grasps for meaning. What's going on? Where am I? To my right, and a little behind me, my ten-year-old grandson's presence appears. Turning to face Max, my surroundings dissolve into nothing. My breath quivers as a shiver climbs my spine. Just the two of us exist.

Together we are in a bubble outside of space and time detached from anything else. He stands slumped and sweaty as if he had been playing hard and been overtaken by tiredness. Though I cannot see anything specifically wrong with him, I know he is compromised in some way. Concern falls over me like an illness and I hear myself say, "This is not good!" Shuffling my feet in the Canadian soil, the rest of me is far away with my grandson.

A second emotion, even more perplexing than the first, surfaces as I hear the fear in my inner voice: "He could die!" My heart aches to reach out and hug Max. Glacier Lake starts coming into focus. The sun's rays reflecting off the lake temporarily blind me. I close my eyes to maintain contact with him. Love and concern begin pushing and pulling at each other, becoming a flurry of somersaults. Then a deep and powerful resonance of love prevails and I hear my confidence return with words firmly challenging the invisible menace threatening my grandson: "I trust he is safe." Rooted in reassurance and faith, the energy in these words washes over us—for Max is still with me—and fills the bubble surrounding us. Transfixed, we stand together. The breeze shifts the branches above me and my eyes become bathed in light.

With a long, slow inhale, I return fully to my body as the campsite, lake, and sky fill my senses. As I focus, I realize I am facing in the direction of Nevada, where my grandson and his parents live. I pat down my pockets for my phone. I must give them a call. An ironic chuckle gurgles at my throat. My phone is in my car back at the landing and it will be another three days before I get there. What can I do?

Closing my eyes, I focus on opening my heart to the joy and abundance of love. A warm sensation fills my chest. The heart's wisdom merges with my mind forming a prayer:

Dear Max, I wrap you in the gentle cloak of love and health. May all that is to be, be only that of good, and for your greatest and highest well-being. May you hear these words and know that you are safely embraced in love and care.

With all the energy and power I can muster, I raise my arms to the gleaming sun and send this special message to Max.

Staring out at the lake I wonder, Is there anything more I can do? My head shakes from side to side in response. Here in the wilderness, prayer is all I have. It will have to be enough. I reassure myself that Max is in good hands and I have done all that I can. Back at the cooking area, hungrily, I begin preparing dinner.

Tomorrow I start canoeing back. During the remaining time I plan to continue savoring every moment of being alone here in my own special sanctuary.

Despite beautiful scenery, the intermittent rains keep me present to the day-to-day activities of living outdoors. Each of the nine portages between lakes is slippery and soggy. They require all my attention to safely cross with the packs and canoe.

Two days have now passed since my return and five since my visit with Max. It is Friday afternoon and I have just gotten home from running errands. Hearing the door open, David calls to me: "Come here, I have some news." I join him in the den.

"Yes?"

"First, sit down." Concern registers in his voice.

"It's about Max, isn't it?" I ask. In that instant my experience with Max floods my mind.

"Max is sick. Kimberly took him to the doctor. He has swine flu. Todd just called while he was driving home from picking up their prescriptions. All three of them must take the medication and stay home for three days."

Before I call Kimberly, I quickly tell him what had happened the previous Sunday. When Kim's voicemail answers I decide to leave a message that includes briefly sharing my experience with Max and my concern for his health.

When she calls back, she tells me her mother had said, "Kim, my gut is telling me you need to take Max to the doctor now. Don't wait!" Kimberly admits she had been thinking of waiting another day. Fortunately, she followed her mom's advice.

I am glad Max and I had this special telepathic meeting. In that moment I knew that he was at risk. Something out of the ordinary was happening to him. And I was able to wrap him in a blanket of love and care. I did the only thing I knew to do: to send him a prayer to let go of my own fear and to trust that all would be well. And it is: Max has recovered and is doing great! Perhaps in some way I helped Max have the strength he needed to ward off the worst of the swine flu. And perhaps his Nana listened to her gut and took action because she, too, had heard my prayer.

IN ADDITION TO INTUITIVE OR TELEPATHIC MESSAGES, there are inner messages called **directives** that people interpret as coming to them specifically from a deceased loved one, an angel, or God. Directives speak to our souls with messages that don't seem to have originated within us. With proper discernment, which will be discussed in more depth later, they are often interpreted as meant-to-be messages that provide specific direction or guidance, as evidenced by the following events experienced by one woman after her husband's unexpected death.

Drive-by Directive

Peggy's husband died unexpectedly of a heart attack at age fifty-eight during Good Friday church services. Having had no warning of John's weak heart, Peggy was unprepared for the loss and grieved deeply in the first year after his death.

One night, she dreamed she was standing on a street corner with her sister, waiting for a bus, when she began to cry. Her sister asked her what was wrong.

Peggy replied, "Johnny is gone and he went so fast that I had no time to tell him I loved him one last time." The next morning, as she sat alone in her kitchen, the memory of the dream brought fresh tears to her eyes. She decided to get out of the house to take her mind off her grief. As she wandered among various stores in a nearby mall, she heard a voice in her head say, "Turn and look." She obeyed and saw a red sports car on display in the center of the mall. John loved red sports cars; he gave one to each of their two children when they graduated from high school. Peggy then looked at the customized license plates, which read "LOVEJB." J.B. were John's initials. She felt that he was telling her, "I know you love me, and our love will never die."

A second license plate incident convinced Peggy that the first sign from Johnny was not just a coincidence. It happened soon after the death of John's father, who had been especially devastated by his son's passing at so young an age. As Peggy was driving to her father-in-law's funeral, she stopped at a traffic light and glanced at the car next to her. The license plate read "IAMJRB." This time, her husband's full initials jumped out at her. Her sister-in-law also saw the license plate and interpreted it the same way Peggy did: that John was with them in spirit at his father's funeral. A few days later, another sister saw the car with the same license plates.

The night before the first anniversary of her husband's death, Peggy was in bed and nearly asleep when she noticed a brilliant white light streaming into her room and felt its radiating heat. That night John appeared to Peggy in a dream. He was standing in front of a bank of windows, and a bright shaft of light beamed through the glass. He was smiling and happy. Peggy extended her arms toward him but could not reach him. He then said, "I really want you to come see the baby," and was gone. Peggy then found herself in a room with three circles, like a three-ringed circus. The circle closest to her contained Peggy's sister's family. In the far circle was a group of people unknown to Peggy. In the middle circle was a cradle with a beautiful baby girl, her head bathed in dark, curly hair.

When Peggy awoke, she wasn't sure what the dream meant. But the meaning became clear two days later, on Easter Sunday, when she and her two grown children visited John's gravesite. As they stood together in the cemetery, Peggy's son took a cassette recorder out of his pocket and played a special message for his mother: It was the voice of his wife's obstetrician announcing that after nine years of trying, the couple were going to be parents. The family was sure the baby would be a girl, because "John told them so, and he never lied." Eight months later, the family's first grandchild was born—a beautiful baby girl with dark, curly hair.

Peggy's experience demonstrates how both a directive and dreams can help a grieving loved one not only *be* comforted but *be* happy once again.

———————————

THESE AND OTHER MEANT-TO-BE MOMENTS TRANSCEND the realm of mere coincidence. Often these messages are received when we most need to hear them, and they have the power to make everyday occurrences inspired. It's as if a Divine dialogue is taking place, with God communicating with us through synchronicities, signs, dreams, and directives. The more attentive we are to such moments, the more often we realize they're happening to us and to others around us. These events are, in fact, universally experienced within a variety of cultures and beliefs, especially in the case of thin places.

CHAPTER 2

Thin Places:
Finding the Divine
in Difficult Times

WHEN A MEANT-TO-BE MOMENT BECOMES A PROVIDENTIAL opportunity for *being* comforted, peaceful, filled with hope and affirmed in faith, it also can be called a "thin place," where we experience God's loving presence, even in the midst of the most difficult times in our lives.

Although thin places are often experienced as positive, even miraculous events, some of the most transformational ones occur after the devastating death of loved ones, as happened for Lonnie when she lost her four-year-old son:

Tuesday, June 11, 1991, was a beautiful late spring day in Minnesota. School had just let out the previous week for my daughter Amie (twelve) and my son Scott (ten), so we were all looking forward to doing some fun activities together with our preschoolers Brett (four) and Abby (two) over summer vacation. It was warm that day, so we decided to pack a lunch and go to the beach after picking Brett up from vacation Bible school at noon.

It was a picture-perfect day. The kids swam, played in the sand, and climbed on the playground equipment all afternoon. They were reluctant to leave until I told them we needed to go home and eat dinner so we could go watch their daddy play cowboy polo that night at the Washington County Fairgrounds. My husband, Mark, played cowboy polo, which is similar to broomball but on horse-back, with a group of friends from his saddle club.

Mark stopped home after work, towing his horse in the trailer, to eat and change clothes before going to the fairgrounds. The kids were really excited about having a horse in their drive-way and brought carrots out to feed to him. As Mark was getting ready to leave, Brett walked behind the truck and jumped on the trailer with-out Mark seeing him. When Mark pulled out of the driveway and stopped at the corner, Brett tried to jump off and was run over by the trailer. The para-medics arrived just minutes after receiving our 911 call and tried desperately to save Brett, but he died in the ambulance on the way to Regions Hospital in St. Paul. Brett left this world just seven weeks before his fifth birthday.

Brett was a typical little boy. He loved playing in his sandbox and riding his "big bike," so proud that he was getting close to riding without the training wheels. He loved playing with Legos, Ninja Turtles and real turtles, and Rusty, our Sheltie. Brett had recently gone to Kindergarten Round-Up and was practicing writing his name. Just hanging out with his siblings and neighbor friends was his favorite thing to do. He had blond hair, blue eyes, and a beautiful smile.

The next several days were a blur as we prepared to do the unthinkable and make funeral arrangements for Brett. We somehow managed to get through the visitation and funeral, but the reality just wouldn't sink in. How could Brett really be gone? Why did this terrible accident happen? We struggled with the "what if's" and the "if only's" and wished with all our hearts that we could only have the chance to start that day over again.

A friend told us about The Compassionate Friends, a support group for bereaved parents, and Mark and I joined the St. Paul chapter just weeks after the funeral. We found this group to be a lifesaver for us. Just sharing our feelings with others who were experiencing the same things helped us immensely in coping with the loss of Brett.

In the last two days of his life, Brett made a few art projects in vacation Bible school that we treasure for the messages they contained to console us. On Monday he made a cloud out of construction paper. On the cloud he had written, "God loves Brett," and glued rainbow-colored strips outlined in sequins, seeds, and other odds and ends. The second project was a windsock with the words "Trust in God." The messages in these precious pieces brought comfort and hope to our broken hearts.

During that first summer, as I struggled to cope with Brett's physical absence, rainbows continued to appear. Sometimes I saw them in the sky after a rain, or in the mist of the spray of the garden hose. Playing with the hose was something Brett was always fascinated with; maybe he was mesmerized by rainbows, too. Other times I'd spot rainbows on greeting cards, children's books, and packages of Skittles, Brett's favorite candy. Whenever I saw a rainbow of any kind, I felt a sense of calm and peace. I felt they were a sign from God that Brett was okay. But my most cherished rainbow will always be the "God loves Brett" project he made in vacation Bible school on that June day so long ago. It reminds me of God's unfailing love, and his promise that Brett is in heaven, safe in the arms of Jesus, where we all will be reunited some day.

Journaling was very therapeutic for me. I often put my feelings into letters to Brett. One of the letters reads:

Dear Brett,
It takes both sunshine and rain to make a rainbow. I think of you as the sunshine in our lives, and the rain is the terrible accident that took you away from us. You brought so much love and joy in your four-and-a-half

years with us, and you touched so many hearts. You will forever be our "little buddy." We love you and miss you so much.

On June 11, 2004, thirteen years to the day after Brett went to heaven, my grandmother Grace lost her battle with breast cancer. That afternoon there was a thunderstorm, and of course I was searching the sky for a rainbow after the storm had passed.

Yes, I did see a rainbow...a beautiful double rainbow!

—LONNIE BOHNEN

LONNIE'S STORY ABOUT HER SON BRETT POIGNANTLY ILLUS-trates that heartfelt longing we often have after the death of a loved one. We pray for a joyful reunion with them in the next world, yet we yearn to feel that we are still close to them on earth. We want signs that reassure us that they're at peace, but still present in our lives. Such signs belong to a unique category of meant-to-be events called "thin places."

In the Celtic tradition, a thin place is an intense spiri-tual connection to a geographic location (such as Ireland) or to the ancient people who once lived there. But espe-cially when they occur just before, during, or after a death, thin places are meant-to-be experiences in which we feel we have encountered the Divine in the space between this world and the next. Theologian Marcus Borg describes thin places in *The Heart of Christianity: Rediscovering a Life of Faith:*

> There are minimally two layers or dimensions of reality, the visible world of our ordinary experiences, and God, the sacred Spirit. "Thin places" are places where these two levels of reality meet or intersect, where the veil momentarily lifts and we behold God, experience the one in whom we live, all around us and within us.

Thin places can be experienced in any moment that we feel embraced by the Holy. But especially in the midst of tragedy and loss, the significance of thin places can be felt in a special relationship, the magnificence of nature, or an unexpected sign that has the power to comfort and calm us just when we need it most.

The end of life is a profound thin place, when the veil is nearly transparent. Often the dying person, and sometimes others who are present, perceive what lies beyond the physical dimension of earthly life. Sometimes the revelation comes through our loved ones' last words, perhaps some variation on "it's so beautiful here." One dying woman weakly, but enthusiastically, proclaimed, "Wow, this is *great!*" just before taking her last breath. Even those who don't die peacefully sometimes seem to experience a thin place during their final moments. A hospice nurse noticed this when an elderly man, who had angrily resisted death, apparently witnessed the white light observed by others who reported near-death experiences and then shouted, "Will someone turn that damn light off!"

Several stories in this chapter describe thin-place moments that occurred just before or after the death of a loved one. The next story is not unlike Lonnie's account about the significance of rainbows after the death of her son and her grandmother.

Moira's Journey

Patricia's story is also about the loss of a child and the thin places she and others witnessed in the hours before and after her daughter died:

> At the age of ten, Moira was diagnosed with juvenile onset diabetes. She was considered an uncontrolled, brittle diabetic and developed problematic health issues in her late twenties. Our reaction to these consequential complications was to be aggressive, to get caught up in rescuing her, and, essentially, turn Moira over to the medical professionals. By 1997, at age thirty-four, our daughter's life had been placed in the hands of the transplant doctors at a Minneapolis hospital. Unfortunately, in spite of two previous body organ transplants, the quality of her life never significantly improved. The shadow of suffering followed her.
>
> On Oct. 24, 2003, Moira began to live out her last days on the transplant floor at the hospital. She

had been admitted with renal failure, a cluster of viruses, severe shingles, and paralysis of her extremities. Her transplant physician immediately encouraged a live-donor kidney transplant. Her brother, Sean, became that contributor. His gift had the potential for giving Moira a decent quality of life.

Moira longed to be happy and to live a normal life. She prayed she would become free of her medical bondage and dreamed of marrying her soul mate, Steve. When Sean's vital gift of his kidney was realized, some of the layers of insecurity and emptiness Moira had experienced in her medically intense world were restored. In fact, Sean's offering of his kidney transformed both Moira and Sean. For Moira, it was proof that she was loved.

Barely a month after Moira's final kidney transplant, she was diagnosed with widespread posttransplant lymphoproliferative disorder. This cancer, surrounding many of her organs, had progressed virtually unnoticed by her physicians during the months Moira laid motionless in her hospital bed. The cause of this cancer was a cumulative effect from years of maintenance suppression. The transplant doctors promptly assured us that this particular type of lymphoma was responsive to certain "smart" drugs and readily treatable. Ironically, Moira's brother's transplanted kidney was working perfectly even without anti-rejection drugs.

But by Ash Wednesday, five months after her initial admittance to the hospital, Moira had taken a turn for the worse. She had difficulty breathing and was hemorrhaging profusely. She was immediately transferred to the intensive care unit.

On Wednesday of Holy Week, Moira was in agony, her body and soul engulfed in pain. She had developed severe pressure sores on her sacrum and her left foot. Her breathing was perilous. We witnessed the horrific shutting down of Moira's organs, including her cherished kidney recently given by her brother. She was moved to hospice care on Holy Thursday, April 8, 2004.

By the time Moira reached the Our Lady of Good Counsel Home (now Our Lady of Peace Home) her condition was grave and deteriorating quickly. Immediately, six Missionaries of Charity sisters from Calcutta, who were visiting the hospice, circled Moira's bed. All were garbed in their traditional flowing white and blue-trimmed saris. They displayed a reverence for Moira's life by their actions, care, respect, and gentleness. In their sacred way, they were respectfully administering to her as a dying human being. The sisters braided her hair, dressed her in a silk gown, and mercifully hid all necessary medical access equipment. Moira's forehead was no longer creased with pain and her face displayed a mystical peace. This was the end of her arduous journey and these special servants of God were sending her home. During this sacrament of her death, Moira's soul had been given the opportunity to take its leave with dignity and serenity. On April 8, 2004, around 8 p.m., she was born to life eternal at the young age of forty-one years and twenty-three days, approximately eight hours after her arrival at hospice.

In the moment of Moira's death, the heavens provided a magnificent sunset flooding the western sky, displaying an assortment of brilliant colors with incredible energy. The delicacy of the purples, pinks, golds, and oranges appeared especially vibrant in the essence that sun, dust, and dancing crystals create. This vivid and blessed image nourished our grieving spirits.

On Good Friday, the day after her death, Native American Indian rituals were dedicated to Moira amid the towering redwood trees in the middle of the Quaker Retreat Center in California. Twenty-four young medical students gathered for class presentations on Native American healing practices. Their professor, Dr. Lewis Mehl-Madrona, was the coordinator for the program of integrative medicine at the University of Arizona in Tucson.

One of the participating medical students was Moira's cousin, Marcia, who had just received word that Moira had died. Moira was the first in their generation to die. Marcia's sadness was noticed by Dr. Mehl-Madrona, who asked if she would share the nature of her sorrow. Following her response, he asked if it would be agreeable to dedicate the afternoon and evening ceremonies to Moira. The rituals would symbolically emphasize a lesson regarding death, rebirth, and viewing people and the world with reverence.

Prayers were offered to assist Moira in her passing over to the spirit world, the beginning of her journey back to the eternal place. Requests were made that Moira spend a few moments with them. Moira responded. Her spirit appeared present in time and space, as was witnessed by a number of the participants. Powerfully visible apparitions of Moira's presence, with her late father, emerged in the mist above and among the giant redwood trees.

Members of the medical student group were able to see specific points in Moira's life, such as seeing a dog and a young girl with straight blond hair and an ID bracelet. During her childhood, Moira had pet dachshunds, was diagnosed with diabetes at age ten, and wore diabetic identification information around her wrist. Dr. Mehl-Madrona stated that Moira indicated to him that she loved her freedom in the spirit world after being so constricted on earth.

The ceremony and ritual for Moira, in Muir Woods where Moira had visited during a vacation some years before, provided clues to mind-body connections and the integral part each plays in the healing process. It instilled association of the relationship of spiritual awareness to soul-linked medicine. It fostered belief that all that happened in Muir Woods that day happened for a reason, that it was meant to be.

The writings of Irish philosopher John O'Donohue relate that the veil separating heaven and earth is very thin and that we mortals can be given a glimpse into the eternal world. He believed that those who now live in heaven are able to come to meet us, to bring us home, and give the one they come for great strength, support, and encouragement. The two worlds touch when a deceased loved one communicates and comes back to be present in this particular time and space. We sensed that Moira's dad came for his beloved daughter while her youngest brother, Patrick, admired exceptional rays of light at daybreak on Holy Thursday. The momentary lifting of veils, exposing a closeness of the Divine and earthly, were further made known by the breathtaking beauty of the skies during Moira's passing, as witnessed by medical students, and visions of Moira with her father during their physician-guided visit into the spiritual realm.

Moira's spirit lives on, even though her human presence in the world has vanished. The darkness of her suffering is over. Moira, who demonstrated such great courage, will forever be a part of our very beings. She is peacefully home in the loving hands of God.

—PATRICIA HAGGERTY, MOIRA'S MOM

I N ADDITION TO *being* COMFORTED AND HAVING THEIR faith affirmed, Patricia and Lonnie's stories demonstrate how sunsets and rainbows are powerful opportunities for *being* awed by nature's grandeur. Nature is a profound thin place, especially when manifested in glorious events that seem Divinely orchestrated. The timeliness of witnessing such beauty in the midst of so much pain provided reassurance of a loving Creator who has now welcomed the mothers' beloved children into their new home.

EVENTS THAT TRIGGER THE PROFOUND INSIGHT OR UNDER-standing of a thin place can be dramatic or miraculous in nature. This is particularly true for incidents that occur immediately after the death of a loved one.

Messages from Mikey

Carol received similar "messages" from her oldest son, Mikey, soon after he died while on a camping trip with college friends in the mountains of Colorado. Mikey's buddy was driving his truck on a quiet mountain road when the vehicle hit a partially buried boulder, which caused the truck to roll off the edge. Mikey, seated in the front, was killed instantly. He was twenty years old.

Hours later, at 4:30 a.m., a police officer, accompanied by a paramedic and chaplain, rang the doorbell at the home of Mikey's parents in St. Paul, Minnesota. As soon as they learned the identity of their visitors, they knew something horrible had happened. Carol assumed their youngest son, Joey, who had attended his high school's homecoming dance earlier that evening, had been in an accident. But Joey was already home and in bed.

When they learned that Mikey was dead, his shocked parents woke up Joey, and they sat together in gut-wrenching pain as the minister said a quick prayer before leaving.

Numbed by their loss, the family felt their grief eased by meant-to-be "signs" from Mikey that Carol says arrived almost immediately. She had been told to watch for the signs by a friend who had lost his wife a few years earlier. "The signs will come, fast and furious," he said. "Write them down so you don't forget them." The signs were a "Godsend" that Carol says saved her during the first days of her grief.

Mikey loved music. He had a part-time job as a DJ and was especially intrigued by song lyrics. A favorite song of Mikey and his family was John Denver's "Rocky Mountain High," which they played whenever they traveled to Colorado for ski trips. Mikey also loved his Minnesota Twins cap and was rarely seen without it. A few months earlier, his aunt had given him a new cap to replace the old one. Assuming Mikey had thrown out the old cap, Carol asked his Colorado friends to look for the new hat, and to send it to her if they found it. It was such a special remembrance of her precious son.

While the family was at the mortuary, friends and neighbors waited at the house, preparing food and listening to music on the CD player. During that time a package was delivered. When she returned home, Carol opened the box, gasping as she pulled out Mikey's newer Twins cap. The family passed the beloved memento around, sniffed it, and unanimously agreed it "smelled like Mikey." A friend then exclaimed, "Listen! Do you hear the song playing right now? Mikey is talking to you!" It was John Denver's tune "My Sweet Lady."

The popular song can be heard via YouTube videos with John Denver singing it, for those who don't remember the lyrics. The singer is speaking to a grieving lady, asking why she is crying and reminding her that they will always be together, entwined in love.

As Carol listened to the words, she noticed the sun's warm rays shining through the bay window of their kitchen. Until that moment, the day had been overcast and gloomy; now Carol felt Mikey's spirit brightening the room. "He's here, I know he's here!" she exclaimed.

Feeling the warmth of the sun, receiving Mikey's hat, and hearing the song all within the same moment convinced Carol and everyone else that her son—and God—was sending a sign to comfort her. Their certainty was affirmed two days later by another thin-place moment. As the family was picking out photos to show at Mikey's wake, the CD player was on yet again, playing a host of songs on full random shuffle. The doorbell rang, and at that instant the family once again heard the song "My Sweet Lady." Carol's husband opened the door to find a small box at his feet. He picked it up and turned to Carol with it in his arms. She exclaimed, "Open the box!" Mike cut it open as Carol heard the lyrics affirming how close loved ones still are to each other. She reached inside and pulled out Mikey's original Twins hat. To this day Carol doesn't know who sent this cherished reminder of her son, but she has no doubt that somehow her son was behind it. The song had played each time the two treasured hats arrived.

The inner messages and other signs that continue to bring her comfort enable Carol to say, "I no longer just *believe* there's a God, I *know* it!" On the third anniversary of Mikey's death, she wrote a memorial that ends with four lines of words her son communicated directly to her:

Three years have gone by
since you passed over into Heaven.
We have learned many things since that time.
We know Heaven must be close because we feel
your love every day.
Your signs give us strength and hope
In knowing one day we will all be
Together again in Paradise.

Open your heart
& know God is love.
God & Heaven are everywhere.
Always Remember: Love never dies!

Winged Clouds

Thin-place experiences reinforce the idea that love lives on after those we have loved have died. Writer Becky Henry made that discovery on the fiftieth birthday of her dear friend Kim, who died before she could celebrate that landmark event. This time, however, the triggering events presented themselves to one person only:

> Paddling my bright yellow kayak quietly around the little lake my cabin sits on in northern Wisconsin, I silently wished my friend Kim a happy fiftieth birthday. It was July 7, 2007, and as always, I remembered her birthday from the little hand-painted plate that sat in her china cabinet with her birthdate of July 7, 1957, painted carefully under her name. This one was special, fifty years, and on such a cool date—7/7/07— one she had wanted so badly to live to see.
>
> Kim was one of the bravest people I ever met. She was diagnosed with stomach cancer and given about four months to live just before Christmas 1997. I learned the news at the rehearsal for the Sunday school Christmas program one cold Saturday morning. She was there, as always, with her three young kids, to prepare for the program. During a break I searched her out and gave her a big hug and we quietly wept. Her mom had died some twenty years before of the same cancer, so we knew the prognosis was grim.
>
> Millions of prayers and amazing tenacity, mixed with some creative medical care, kept Kim with us for four more years. She volunteered at school with her chemo fanny pack, went to Hawaii many times with her family, and enjoyed life as much as possible. Sometimes it seemed she wasn't even sick she

lived life so fully. Kim continued working as a dental hygienist for as long as her body allowed.

She wasn't afraid of dying. She spoke so openly about it that it seemed natural, even refreshing. Sure, she had her down times, especially when she talked with a group of us about her kids being without her at such young ages. That tore her up more than anything. I'll never forget her telling us, her bright blue eyes spilling over with tears, about her daughter lying with her in bed and crying as she asked her why she had to be sick. Kim wrote long letters to each of her kids to be given to them after she was gone.

Toward the end of Kim's fight with cancer, my daughter became seriously ill with a life-threatening eating disorder, which sent me into a state of constant fear and panic. One day after my daughter's first hospitalization, I received a funny card from Kim about banging your head on the floor when life got to be frustrating. She wrote a long encouraging note, one of the few I received during that time. I could hardly believe it. Here this woman was dying of cancer, leaving behind three small children, yet she took the time to brighten my day. I still shake my head in amazement.

One cold February day I called Kim to find out her secret to staying so strong. I had spent the day before in bed, not able to get out, feeling overwhelmed and simply frozen with fear. There seemed to be nothing I could do to help my daughter; she had just recently overdosed and was still suicidal.

"What do you mean, my secret for staying strong?" Kim asked.

I told her how amazed I was that she continued to go on with her life as if nothing was wrong. Going to Hawaii, volunteering at school and church, driving the kids to sporting events, and socializing like she always had—it all just blew me away.

After denying that she had a secret, Kim shared with me what really kept her going. "Becky, when I'm having a bad day or feeling down and sad," she said, "I let myself have a good cry and then I say, 'Come on, Kim, you've got to do this.' And that is how I keep going."

My mouth hung open. "That's it? You just have a good cry and give yourself a pep talk and then you go on?"

"That's what I do."

"Well, okay, then," I said, and I went and got into the shower and sat on the floor and cried for half an hour while the water washed away my tears. I did feel better after I told myself, "Come on, you've got to do this." It was some of the kindest, most sincere and helpful advice anyone gave me during that crisis. When I would start to feel sorry for myself again and think I had it pretty tough, I would think of Kim and it gave me a whole new perspective: I wasn't dying. I was healthy and strong and able to be there to try to help my daughter get well.

In May 2002, on a Sunday after attending the confirmation of the group of boys she mentored, Kim went to heaven. She had decided long before that when her quality of life no longer allowed her to participate, she would let go. And she did. She met her last commitment and then she went into a coma and went on to the next place. After the funeral, her women friends made one big margarita and shared it in a toast to our extraordinarily brave and generous friend.

Now, as I was slowly paddling my way around the lake that beautiful summer morning, I noticed that there was not one single cloud in sight. I thanked Kim for her steadfast support and love in my darkest days. I wished Kim a happy birthday again, out loud this time. "We'll have a toast to you later today when we're out for our pontoon ride at sunset," I said to Kim and the cloudless sky.

As I paddled around the curve of the lake, I looked up again. This time I saw a huge, beautiful, dancing angel cloud straight in front of me. I couldn't believe my eyes. "Kim, is that you? Thank you for letting me know you heard my wishes for you." After staring and blinking, I began to doubt what I'd just seen.

"Maybe I've lost it," I quietly said to myself. "Maybe the stress of living with this eating disorder all these years has finally gotten to me. What a nice little fantasy, to think that my friend came to visit me from heaven. But people are going to think I'm nuts if I tell them about this." I resolved not to say a word and just enjoyed the thought that I had been visited from the next place. Then, as I paddled around the next curve of the lake, I gasped out loud as yet another cloud appeared. This time it was two enormous angel wings! I laughed, and at the same time tears rolled down my face, "It was you, wasn't it? I doubted, and you wanted to show me that it really was you! Thank you, Kim! This is the best birthday party ever."

No one else was on the lake that morning, not even the fishermen who were usually out for their morning casting. I was completely alone, or so I'd thought. Of course I didn't have a camera with me and no one else saw those amazing clouds. But the experience filled my soul with joy and gratitude. I smiled and smiled as I picked up my paddle and continued on my journey around the lake. There were no more clouds that hot July day, just a heart brimming with the love of a heaven-sent friend.

—BECKY HENRY

A Cautionary Stranger

Like Becky, Wendell was alone when he experienced an innocuous thin-place moment. Unlike Becky, Wendell was with others when he experienced a second thin-place moment that could be called miraculous. Both moments "coincidentally" involved deer.

One night several years ago, Wendell, an art professor at a small midwestern college, was driving his sports car along a deserted, winding road in rural Wisconsin. A deer suddenly jumped in front of the car from a ditch, striking the left fender and hood. After pulling over to check on the deer, Wendell attempted to pull the damaged piece of fender away from the tire it was rubbing against.

As Wendell struggled, a man appeared in front of the car's headlights. This seemed odd to Wendell because the accident occurred in a remote area, without homes or farms within several miles. The man had no car.

The stranger asked, "Did you hit a deer?" Wendell admitted he had, to his dismay, and mentioned how upset he was about the accident. The man then asked, "Do you know the intersection approximately three-quarters of a mile ahead?" When Wendell said he did, the man continued, "You were fortunate to have stopped. Less than a minute ago a car ran the stop sign of the intersection traveling more than eighty miles per hour." How the man could have been at that particular intersection a minute earlier baffled Wendell. He turned to give the fender another pull or two, and then rose to thank the man. But he was gone, disappearing into the night as quickly as he had arrived.

When Wendell described this angel-like appearance at a chapel service at the college where he teaches, he shared its impact: "This event was clear and real, including the death of the deer and the cost of the repairs. As I stand before you this morning I cannot give you an explanation, but it has continued as an important message that has lived with me for the past twenty-five years."

Dual Deer Visits

A second encounter with deer served to reaffirm not only Wendell's faith, but also that of his family during one of the most tragic times in their lives.

Wendell's nephew Paul was a sensitive, caring nineteen-year-old, headed toward a wonderful life of service to others, when he died in a car accident in Iowa. Following his funeral, Wendell and his wife joined the procession of cars headed to the country cemetery several miles from the church. When the cars neared the graveyard, five deer appeared in a field to the right. The deer then ran parallel to the line of cars and, approaching the hearse, four of them jumped the fence and stood in the middle of the road. The procession came to a halt. Meanwhile, the fifth deer remained to the right, staring at the hearse. The four deer then crossed the road. Although the fifth one followed, it first stood briefly in front of the hearse, staring at its occupants as if it knew them. Finally, the deer joined its companions on the far embankment, where all five watched as the procession continued to the cemetery.

After the burial ceremony, Wendell and his wife were returning home when the same scene repeated itself. Twenty or so deer were in a field to the west when five broke away and crossed the road immediately in front of their vehicle, in the same sequence of four, then one.

Paul's mother had prayed throughout the previous evening for a sign to find some sense, some peace and reassurance in her grief and loss. For her and the entire family, their prayers were answered in the behavior of the five deer—incidentally, the same number of people in Paul's immediate family. Those experiences triggered a comforting thin place moment for that family in its hour of despair.

A Late Gift

For Marlene King, it was a much-belated Christmas gift from her father that later conveyed the message she most wanted to receive:

> Christmas was always special to our family, and I was looking forward to a holiday season that promised to be our best one yet. Our business was beginning to thrive after a long struggle, and I had just had a wonderful visit with my dad that meant a lot to us both. Life was indeed good.
>
> A few weeks before Christmas, I received a call at my work desk just prior to leaving to meet my sister-in-law for her birthday celebration lunch. The words from the doctor on the other end of the line ran together, but eventually I made sense of what he was saying: my father had died of a massive heart attack while he was at work. After tears and screams of denial, I found myself on a flight to San Diego. An only child, it was up to me to help with all that happens after a sudden death—most

of which dealt with the practical logistics for my mother, who had never even written a check.

I put my grief on hold while I worked quickly to sort out overwhelming details; I had only a short amount of time I could be away from home and my business without creating a hardship for my husband. It took six full days around the clock to sort through my father's inventory of rare books and collectibles, figure out his loosely kept personal and business accounting methods, and make an assessment of the sixty years of his private correspondence and keepsakes. I called an estate auctioneer and made arrangements to sell what I could and retained the most valuable pieces for my mother to keep and deal with later. Exhaustion was not an option as I put the final touches on a budget plan for my mother to follow. Feeling I had done as much as I could, I returned home.

Upon my arrival, my husband said a package had arrived from my parents. My dad had mailed our Christmas gifts before his death. A bittersweet feeling of joy and sorrow washed over me. After decorating the tree, we carefully unpacked the wrapped packages from my parents and placed them underneath the tree. I noticed several were from my dad to me, just like always.

Christmas morning found us opening presents, as I attempted to find gratitude and excitement in the generous and wonderful gifts from friends and family. I saved my dad's gifts until last. There was a small mother-of-pearl inlaid box made from olive wood, a red leather jewelry box, a pink snuggly warm robe, and a pant and blouse outfit with a washcloth tucked between the two pieces. I thought this was odd, but my dad had an unusual sense of humor. The washcloth had a frog printed on it and I could only wonder what on earth this meant to him, as it was nothing I'd ever use! He knew I had French provincial taste and decor, so I placed the washcloth in my linen cabinet and decided I would always keep it to remind me of him.

We celebrated many Christmases after that, but they were never quite the same. Life became busier. During a move to another city over Thanksgiving weekend one year, I found a box marked "linens" and pulled out the froggy washcloth from my dad along with some towels. I decided this would be a good time to initiate it. My dad would have loved our new house and location, and I wished he were there to enjoy it with us.

The hot water in the shower felt so good, since I was dirty, tired, and my muscles ached from a long day of hauling boxes, organizing, and putting things away. I rinsed the washcloth in the hot water and held it to my face, letting the steam seep in. When I went to put it under the showerhead again, I saw there was more than a frog on it: the water had chemically activated a "secret message" on the cloth that read, "I love you."

Tears flooded my eyes. Now everything made sense. My dad was proud of me and I believe he orchestrated and timed his message to reaffirm our connection, even though he was gone.

—Marlene King

—————

It may be that we experience thin-place moments more often in times of tragedy because we are much more open to them. We desperately want to believe in eternal life: that we will be reunited with those we've loved and lost. Thus, ironically perhaps, the most difficult events in our lives can result in the breakdown of barriers to a belief in God. We realize that the signs we observed could not have happened unless something far greater than ourselves enabled them.

There are innumerable ways to experience God's presence in our lives. Many people take comfort in sacred Scripture to help them understand God's message to humankind. Some also find God in their religious traditions, rituals, and faith communities. Others who are deeply spiritual, but perhaps not religious, experience God in nature or in other personal ways. Regardless of our religious beliefs or practices, however, we all can *be* witnesses to the manifestation of Divine Providence when we are mindful of our own spiritual experiences.

CHAPTER 3

The Universality of Meant-to-be Moments

MEANT-TO-BE MOMENTS ARE EXPERIENCED BY PEOPLE from a variety of religious backgrounds and faith traditions, as well as by those who have a hard time believing in a personal God or even that God exists at all. When we listen nonjudgmentally to the stories and interpretations of people's spiritual experiences, friendships become richer and deeper. In sharing these important stories, we learn how God is actively present in all our lives. Some of my closest friends have very different beliefs from my own, yet I've loved sharing our meant-to-be moments with each other. One of the people I've learned most from is my Hindu friend Leela.

Leela's Final Farewell to Her Father

Leela shared this story with me many years ago:

> On May 14, 1998, I called my parents in India to talk to them because the night before I had had a

troubling dream. I dreamt my mother, my older sister, and I went to some event. My mom was wearing
a new sari (a traditional Indian dress worn by most
women) yet she was extremely sad and distraught
and I did not know why. After awakening the next
morning, I was concerned about my mother so
I called my parents to find out if my mother was
feeling well. I had my usual chat with my father
before he handed the phone to my mother. When
I told her about my dream, she was taken aback
because she was wearing a new sari in the dream.
I didn't know it at the time, but later I learnt from
my mother that in some parts of Indian traditions,
when a woman's husband dies, the wife wears a
new sari to the funeral. This is what upset her about
my dream, especially since my father had survived
a massive heart attack some months earlier.

After our conversation ended, I went about my
daily routine. Three days later, as I was sitting and
reading the Sunday paper, the phone rang. It was
my nephew from California calling me. It seemed
odd to me that he was calling me again because
we'd had a long conversation the day before. He
said he had some bad news to tell me: "Grandpa
has died." I cried, "What are you talking about? I
just talked to him on the phone on Thursday and
he was perfectly fine." He repeated the message
again and again, explaining that his father had
phoned him from India to tell him the news. Then
it hit me: My father really had passed away. Later, I

learned from my mother that in her deepest grief she kept recalling the dream I had shared with her three days before.

My father passed away in India on May 17, 1998. The next day my father appeared to me here in Minnesota (I am an intuitive and a Reiki teacher and I do energy work) in his spirit body and stayed with me for the next three days and communicated with me. When he appeared on May 18, his energy felt very strong and powerful to me. I was in such emotional pain that I could not "hear" parts of what he was trying to convey to me, so he appeared in his spirit body to a dear friend. He told her to tell me that he would be spending three days with me, and he would be leaving on May 20 at 3:39 pm.

During the three days he visited with me in his spirit body, my father could see the things in my home. He observed, "This house has a lot of wood in it" (homes in India are not built with wood). Later, when a friend stopped by, my father was surprised at the color of her blond hair because he never had seen blond hair before. He kept saying to me, "Look at the color of her hair!" As my friend and I shared an Indian meal of chapati (a homemade flat bread) and spiced vegetables, my father was surprised that a westerner could eat a spicy meal.

I was in awe of his ability to see and hear so clearly in his spirit body. He was observing everything I was doing and kept asking me questions about it. The lawn needed mowing and he asked,

"Who will mow the lawn?" When I turned on the television, he mentioned how clear the picture was, not like his TV in India, which had very poor reception. He noticed how clean the house was and asked me to open the cupboard so he could see the new contact paper that I had just laid on the shelf. (Since his passing, whenever I open that cupboard, I remember him.)

On May 20 around 11 a.m., I saw in the spirit world an energetic white carpet runner being laid down; it was about 3 feet wide and extended from my front door steps all the way into the sky. Throughout that morning, I saw family members, relatives, my father's friends, and acquaintances who had already passed away before him, lining up on each side of the energetic white carpet runner, as though they were waiting to welcome him to the other side. My eyes filled with tears.

I was saying goodbye to my father when the phone rang. It was my daughter calling to find out if her grandpa's spirit was still there. When I said yes, she raced over to the house and walked in the front door at 3:38 p.m. She said her goodbyes to him through me. At exactly 3:39 p.m. he walked out the front door, stepped onto the energetic white carpet runner, and walked toward the people in their spirit bodies who had lined up on each side waiting to greet him and welcome him. He continued to walk until he disappeared into brilliant white light and I could not see him or the others anymore. All this took place in a few seconds. I feel truly blessed to have been given the gift of witnessing his sacred departure from the physical world to the spirit world.

Not too long after my father had gone into the light, I remembered a conversation I had with him during my visit to India shortly after his heart attack back in March 1997. My father and I had many conversations during that time, including one in which he spoke of just how close he had come to dying. Several times, he repeated the same phrase, "It would have been a glorious departure." At that time, I did not understand the meaning of what he was trying to convey. Now it is crystal clear to me. He had seen a glimpse of what awaited him when he passed on.

It has been over sixteen years since my father made the transition into spirit life. A few years ago, my mother passed away. My father, my older sister, my mother's parents, siblings, cousins, aunts, uncles, her neighbors, and friends gathered to welcome my mother as she entered into spirit life. Once again, I was blessed to witness the grace of her stepping into spirit life and her sacred reunion with my older sister who had passed away just a few years before her. I was in awe of the love between my mother and my sister that continues to live on the other side, beyond the veil.

Since my parents' passing, each and every day without fail, I remember them and call on them for

help in my physical life. Knowing their unconditional love is forever present in my life brings me
enormous comfort and blessing and tears of joy.
Whenever I see number 339 on a car license plate
or on a clock, I "hear" my father speak to me, and I
choke up with the joy of connecting with him. And
now I have similar connections with my mother
too. I think I was given the gift of witnessing the
sacredness of my parents' journey passing on to
spirit life so I can share my stories with others who
have lost their own loved ones and they can receive
comfort and healing, too.

———

LEELA'S THREE-DAY VISIT FROM HER FATHER POWERFULLY
illustrates that meant-to-be moments are found across cultures, in numerous faith traditions and beliefs, from Hin-
duism to Christianity to Judaism and even agnosticism. As
noted earlier, in Judaism, for instance, the word *bashert*,
which means "fated" or "destined," describes what's meant
to be. *Bashert* is typically used to refer to one's preordained
spouse or soul mate; thus, you might hear Jewish singles
say they are looking for their *bashert*, the person who com-
plements them best, the one with whom they are meant
to be. But you will also hear *bashert* used to describe other
meant-to-be experiences.

A Grandfather's Love Never Dies

Dorienne, an Orthodox Jewish woman from South Africa, shared with me several of her *bashert* experiences, most involving her young son and her deceased father:

> My father died just a week before my son Gary was born. The second day in the hospital after giving birth, just toward the end of visiting hours, I heard a cough, which was typical of my father. I walked into the hallway and no one was there. So I asked the nurses if anyone else had been near my room and they assured me the hall had been empty. In that moment, I knew my father had been there to see his grandchild.

Shortly after this, Dorienne had another reassuring experience:

> The night before we moved into our new home, our bed was placed to face the mirror on the dresser. Everything was very quiet. Then we heard the same throat-clearing sound of my father. We looked up and my husband Michael and I saw him clearly in the mirror. We instinctively knew he had come to see where we lived because he had never gotten a chance to see our new home. We were never frightened. I was delighted. It was comforting to know he could see where we now lived.

Dorienne believes her father also has fostered her son Gary's interest in music. When he was about three years old, Gary began singing songs that Dorienne had never taught him. They were songs her father used to sing, songs he had learned during World War II. Once, when Gary was singing "*Whispering*," one of her father's favorites, Dorienne asked Gary who taught him the song. "Grandpa Gus," he replied.

Dorienne also inherited an old ukulele when Gus died. After she had it restored to its original condition, she brought it home. Young Gary picked it up and began to play songs her father once played on the instrument. No other family member knew how to play it. Astonished, Dorienne asked Gary how he had learned to play the songs. Once again, he replied, "Grandpa Gus taught me."

A faith-affirming near-death experience

For Diane, a Roman Catholic, a near-death experience when she was eight caused her to embark on a lifelong spiritual journey, guided by her unshakable belief that some things are meant to be:

> Everything changed for me one beautiful August morning in 1955, the month before I was to start fourth grade. It's easy to pinpoint the exact time because I had a brain hemorrhage that day. I was sitting on the sofa watching *Axel and His Dog*, a popular local children's TV show, and eating red licorice when I got a blinding headache.
>
> My mom was downstairs doing laundry so I

staggered across what instantly seemed like a much larger living room to the basement door, bouncing off the sofa, end table and hallway wall as I went. I had barely enough time to call down to her before my legs buckled beneath me. In the few seconds it took Mom to reach me, I passed out, and she scrambled to the phone for help.

I could hear her screaming out the back door to our next-door neighbors, "Ralph, Florence, come quick, help me, something has happened to Diane." They laid me gently on the bed and waited for what must have seemed like an eternity until the ambulance came. I remember trying to say something to reassure Mom, but I couldn't move a muscle or open my eyes.

I don't recall anything more until I "woke up" to find myself looking down on me—the physical me—lying on an operating table, surrounded by several doctors working to save my life. Although it sounds like it must have been very scary, I had no sense of anxiety or fear, just the comforting knowledge that my body was entirely separate from the "real" me. Even now, I can instantly bring to mind, with great clarity, the profound sense of well-being I experienced during the time I spent in both worlds. That memory has been a comfort to me my entire life.

As I hovered near the ceiling, I could see my mom frantically waiting in another room for news of my condition. I wanted to comfort her, tell her, "Mom, don't worry, I'm just fine," but, instinctively,

I knew I was simply an observer and unable to participate in what was happening.

You may think that what happened to me took place in my imagination, in an anesthetically induced dream state. I wondered too. But God soon gave me proof I hadn't imagined what I remember so vividly.

While I was floating blissfully in the in-between space above my body, I noticed one of the physicians assisting with the surgery. Her sure hands and deft movements mesmerized me. In the '50s, a woman doctor was rare. A Korean woman doctor working in a hospital in St. Paul, Minnesota, was as rare as, say—an out-of-body-experience. Small and soft-spoken, with a slight limp and a broad smile, I instantly recognized her when she came into my room to visit me a few days later. I hadn't dreamt what happened—it was real!

I went to Catholic school and attended Mass every morning. Like my classmates, by the tender age of eight, I'd memorized much of the Baltimore Catechism—the primer of my Catholic faith doctrine. But my faith had been just a word. Defined in the dictionary, faith means "belief without proof." Now I had proof. My out-of-body experience gave me proof—personal knowledge about the eternal me.

So many meant-to-be moments came together that day to save and change my life. Our doctor, Dr. A., was a bowling buddy of my dad's, a member of our church, and the doctor who delivered me. He lived only a few blocks away from our home in Roseville and arrived at the hospital even before the ambulance. A man of deep faith, he went to Mass every morning.

His faith touched every aspect of his life, and on that particular day it touched mine as well. As he raced to the emergency room, something told him I needed a spinal tap. As soon as I arrived, he performed the procedure, right then and there. That must have been the point when, close to death, the real "me" awakened to usher my eternal self to glory. I'm not sure what brought me back—most likely, it was the sight of my mom, and the anguish she so obviously felt at the thought of losing me.

Many years later, at my dad's funeral, Dr. A. told me he felt guided by the Holy Spirit to do a spinal tap on me that day. I have no doubt that is true. Nothing but Divine guidance could compel most physicians to take such extreme measures in the absence of any concrete evidence.

I deeply believe in the power of prayer to change our hearts and bring the word of God close enough for us to hear it. So it doesn't surprise me that someone who took time from his hectic schedule each day to spend time in prayer and meditation would have access to Divine inspiration.

The incredibly brave and rash decision Dr. A. made to follow his own meant-to-be guidance relieved the pressure in my brain and saved my life that morning so many years ago. When I think of the risk he took for me, I am filled with profound gratitude for the value he placed on my life and also with awe at his dedication to his vocation and willingness to follow the promptings of the Spirit.

I was given a great gift that day. Since the moment I looked down on myself in the ER, I have had no fear of death—that fear left me the moment I knew that my body was not me but only a shell that contained my spirit as long as I needed it. I've learned since that an event such as this is called a "touchstone moment" because it remains in your heart—always ready to comfort and sustain you whenever it's needed. And it has.

But I received an even greater gift as well. What happened made me feel that my very survival was meant to be. I overheard enough people whispering in the corridor outside my room to know that most people who had brain hemorrhages died. Today, brain hemorrhages are fatal for more than 25 percent of people suffering them. In the 1950s, they killed nine out of ten victims. Lying in my hospital bed, I had a lot of time to think about my near death experience and that I was still alive. Like Harry Potter, I was the girl "who lived."

Why had God spared my life? Living with that question changed me. At age eight, I was already on a spiritual quest—one that has lasted the rest of my life. My longing to find an answer has led me down roads I might never have chosen without it.

Over the years, I've asked myself countless times, "Is this it? Is this the reason I was spared?" While I've never felt with any certainty that my search was over, I've learned, as Rainer Maria Rilke said in his book, *Letters to a Young Poet*, "Be patient toward all that is unsolved...and try to love the questions themselves.... Live the questions now." And although I still haven't found an answer, I wouldn't change a thing.

An agnostic's experience

Meant-to-be moments aren't the exclusive domain of the religious faithful. Michele, an agnostic, has had her share of such experiences.

Michele began pulling away from her religious roots during the tumultuous '60s, when guitar masses replaced Latin services after the Second Vatican Council modernized the Catholic Church. Until then, she had loved the mysteriousness of her faith but not its dogma or her parochial school education. She took a stand in junior high, choosing to attend public school and to quit Catechism classes. She had no interest in joining another faith community after that. Some four decades later Michele describes herself as a "spiritual citizen," someone who respects and abides by fundamental values of faith and democracy. She also derives a sense of spirituality from nature, identifying with the earth-friendly beliefs of Native Americans.

Michele has witnessed many meant-to-be moments in her life and in the lives of the patients she cares for as a hospice volunteer. But her most comforting meant-to-be experience took place the morning her mother died, less than thirty-six hours after Michele brought her home from the hospital. Throughout that last night, Michele kept the radio on and tuned to her mother's favorite classical music station as she sat vigil. Toward dawn, her mother's breathing became shallower and more sporadic until it simply stopped. At that moment, "Clair de Lune" began to play on the radio. Michele knew the composition by heart: Her father-in-law had played it at her wedding. Through her tears, she knew the music was no coincidence. It was a mother's parting gift to her daughter, a song of joy to ease her sorrow.

HINDUS, JEWS, CHRISTIANS, MUSLIMS—FOLLOWERS OF ALL faiths, and non-followers as well, experience meant-to-be moments. Belief systems aren't necessarily exclusive; sometimes, a person embraces more than one belief system simultaneously. For example, Leela continues to follow the Hindu teachings and practices she grew up with, yet she also has a personal relationship with Jesus and often attends Catholic Mass. Leela also visits a Reform Jewish synagogue when she feels "called" to do so.

This concept of "interspirituality" is described in *The Mystic Heart: Discovering a Universal Spirituality in the World's Religions* by Brother Wayne Teasdale, who introduces the term as "the sharing of ultimate experiences across traditions...the foundation that can prepare the way of a planet-wide enlightened culture, and a continuing community among the religions that is substantial, vital, and creative."

Interspirituality does not aim to eliminate the rich diversity of our world's religious traditions or to create a one-size-fits-all form of spiritual culture. But it does promote the removal of barriers and distrust among people of various religious beliefs to allow greater appreciation of how alike the foundations of our meant-to-be moments are. The Dalai Lama says:

> Because all the world's religious traditions share the same essential purpose, we must maintain harmony and respect among them. This not only benefits the followers of each religion but makes our neighborhoods and countries more peaceful. To do this, we need to understand something about the world's different religions. There are many ways to go about this, but I believe the most effective way is face-to-face dialogue. Let religious and spiritual leaders meet together to discuss and share their experience and practice; let ordinary members of religious communities spend time with each other.

My own interest in the power of sacred stories began long before I became a spiritual director or co-founded Well Within. Surprisingly, it began while working in the corporate world over coffee and lunch with coworkers and clients from a variety of backgrounds. Back then I was the marketing manager for a national consulting firm that facilitated creative problem-solving sessions for Fortune

500 companies to generate ideas for new products and marketing strategies. There I learned how the process of fostering creativity required an open mind willing to challenge assumptions and prejudices. Our facilitators stressed the importance of "looking for the good" among the hundreds of ideas generated during each brainstorming session. Becoming trained in creative problem solving prompted a more intense curiosity about other people's thoughts and ideas—and not just those relating to new pasta products or children's cereals.

I was blessed to work with Jews, Muslims, Protestants, Catholics, and evangelical Christians, as well as individuals who had no religious affiliations, including at least one self-proclaimed agnostic. Growing up in the pre-Vatican '50s and attending Catholic schools, I barely knew any non-Catholics, much less non-Christians, so I welcomed the opportunity to get to know men and women with spiritual backgrounds different from my own. I still say "yes" to my Catholic beliefs and rituals, but I also incorporate practices, including meditation, from other spiritual traditions. Whereas before I may have said "Yes, *but*," I now say, "Yes, *and*."

Likewise, I have witnessed the benefits of healing practices and techniques at Well Within that have their roots in Buddhist, Hindu, and other Eastern spiritual traditions. Our staff constantly hears success stories about these treatments, which complement traditional Western medicine as they help people relax, reduce stress and anxiety, and live as fully as possible with chronic conditions and serious illnesses.

The universality of spiritual experiences has tremendous appeal to anyone seeking personal growth, regardless of religious belief. When we listen compassionately, without judgment, to the deeply personal meant-to-be stories of others, we draw inspiration and hope from them. Our increasingly diverse world provides countless opportunities for developing friendships that can be deepened by sharing not only our sacred stories, including thin-place ones, but also our interpretations of them. As Frederick Buechner writes in *Listening to Your Life:*

> In the long run, the stories all overlap and mingle like search lights in the dark, and my story and your story are all part of each other's too, if only because we have sung together and prayed together and seen each other's faces so that we are at least a footnote at the bottom of each other's stories.

Casual acquaintances can become good friends—perhaps even soul friends, a concept the late poet John O'Donohue portrays so beautifully in his book, *Anam Cara*.

Soul Friendships and Spiritual Experiences

Leela and I have shared many interspiritual experiences over the years, and our friendship has flourished because of the respect we have for each other's religious traditions and spiritual beliefs. Leela has taught me a great deal about spirituality, especially about the importance of listening to the "still, small voice within." She has learned not only to listen but also to respond to the inner voice when it tells her to contact someone, even when not knowing the reason. She does this constantly, which often enables her to act as a channel of God's wisdom and grace for others.

Leela intuitively knows when I need help, often by telling me that her "guides" have advised her that I need her healing techniques to reduce my own stress and anxiety. Other times, she'll give me invaluable advice, just when I need to hear it. Occasionally, she even perceives that my deceased friends or family members, including my parents, are present during our conversations. On rare occasions, special "guests" make an appearance through her.

I recall one of our visits, not long after Leela and I met, when she said St. Francis was in the room with us. I admit I was startled, but I tried to keep an open mind. After all, I was raised by a mother who was a big fan of certain saints, which influenced my own belief that it is possible to ask the saints, including Francis, to intercede on our behalf with God. I like to think of it as if I were asking a friend to put in a good word for me with "the boss" they see on a daily basis. Besides, it wasn't the first time I'd heard of a non-Catholic "borrowing" a saint, especially those patron saints whose powers have universal appeal.

St. Joseph, for example, has become the patron saint for selling homes, whatever the owners' denomination. Take Ginger's neighbors. Although they're Protestants, they eagerly accepted Ginger's offer of a St. Joseph statue to help sell their home, which had been on the market far too long. Since it was winter, the couple buried the statue in the snow. Within ten days, the house was sold. Elated, they returned the statue to Ginger, who cautioned them, "Maybe you should keep it until after the house closes."

They demurred, feeling confident that everything would proceed on schedule. Just before the closing, however, the buyers had trouble with their financing. Ginger's neighbors returned, sheepishly asking to borrow the statue again. The next day, they were told that everything would work out. To this day, they proudly display the statue in their new home.

I was especially intrigued when Leela said she felt a connection to St. Francis, particularly because he's had a special relationship with my family. My mother's father, a surgeon and accomplished wood carver, had such a fondness for St. Francis that he placed a plaster statue of the saint in his front yard. Using a piece of mahogany he received as payment from an impoverished patient, Gramp also carved a beautiful three-foot-high statue of St. Francis that he displayed prominently in his family's living room.

So how was it that Leela knew St. Francis and that he was with us in the room?

"I can see and hear him," she replied. "He's saying something about a pedestal. And it looks like he's trying to write something—perhaps a note to someone?"

I told Leela about my grandfather and the two St. Francis statues, then shared a thin-place experience of my own, one I had not told many people:

"A few years ago, my family moved into a new home and I decided to continue Gramp's tradition of placing a St. Francis statue—on a *pedestal*—in a flower garden in my front yard. Later that same day, I found a note, written years earlier by my now-deceased mother, thanking me for a St. Francis statue I had given her as an anniversary gift. Finding my mother's note on that particular day seemed like more than a mere coincidence. I interpreted it as a sign from her."

I explained to Leela that finding the note was one of several comforting signs I had had from my mother since her death. I told her I felt that God was telling me to pay attention to what I would learn from her.

A few months later, a second experience affirmed Leela's special gifts of perception. We were chatting when Leela suddenly became quiet. After a moment she said, "Mother Teresa is here with us, talking to me in Hindi."

"Well, what is she saying?" I asked, skeptical but curious about this saintly nun whom I greatly admired and had had the good fortune to meet the year before she died.

"She's saying something about that statue of the woman by the front door [of Well Within]." Leela was referring to a life-sized figure of a woman, created by breast cancer survivors and their caregivers, who used papier-mâché molds of parts of their own bodies to form the statue. Her hands cradle a ceramic bowl, whose fountain of water creates a soothing sound as it washes over small stones.

Leela closed her eyes as if praying. Finally, she said, "It looks like Mother Teresa is pouring something into the bowl the woman is holding." Again uncertain how to interpret what she was seeing, Leela asked me, "Do you have any idea what this means?"

I did. I had traveled to Ireland a few months earlier to work on my first book. I stayed at three monasteries, including Mount Melleray Abbey, a sprawling estate built more than one hundred and fifty years ago in a pastoral area of eastern Ireland. I often walked to the nearby town of

Melleray, which contains a grotto where the Blessed Virgin Mary is believed to have once appeared. I had brought holy water from the grotto home to Minnesota with me, fully intending to pour it into the very bowl Leela had seen in her vision, but I kept forgetting to bring the water to the office. Leela was unaware of my trip, much less the holy water.

The next day, I made sure to pour the holy water into the ceramic bowl.

Once I would have been skeptical, perhaps even fearful, of someone who claimed to see or hear deceased souls. But I've learned to appreciate people like Leela who seem to possess psychic gifts that cannot easily or rationally be explained. Scripture reminds us that humankind has been given a variety of gifts, including the ability to heal others:

> To each individual the manifestation of the Spirit is given for some benefit. To one is given through the Spirit the expression of wisdom; to another the expression of knowledge according to the same Spirit; to another faith by the same Spirit; to another gifts of healing by the one Spirit; to another mighty deeds; to another prophecy; to another discernment of spirits; to another varieties of tongues; and to another the interpretation of tongues. But one and the same Spirit produces all of these, distributing them individually to each person as he wishes. (I Cor: 12: 7-11, New American Standard Bible)

This second experience with Leela prompted me to reflect on Mother Teresa, a stunning example of someone who performed daily acts of unconditional mercy, compassion, and love. Mother Teresa did not judge people based on their religion. She taught her Missionaries of Charity Sisters to honor the spiritual beliefs of others. She knew that to Hindus the Ganges River is considered so holy that many elderly people travel long distances to reach the river, especially at the end of their lives. They believe that if they dip their feet into the Ganges at the time of death, they will be saved. Those who are dying lie near the river, seeking the kindness of strangers who might help place their feet in the water before they take their last breaths. Recognizing this important spiritual need for the dying, especially among the "poorest of the poor," Mother Teresa built a hospice on the banks of the Bagmati River, near Katmandu, Nepal. That river eventually flows into the Ganges, so it too is considered a holy place for dying Hindus. Here, the Sisters provide comfort, food, and medicine until they lovingly carry the dying to the river for this final ritual of their faith.

Very few of us can accomplish what Mother Teresa taught us. But as she said, "We cannot all do great things, but we can do small things with great love." Like Mother Teresa, we can honor the religious beliefs and practices of others by listening to their stories and experiences. When we are mindful of the deeply personal and meaningful meant-to-be stories of others, we learn about the many ways God is present in their lives. Then we can appreciate and honor—not just tolerate—those whose religious and spiritual beliefs differ from our own.

My experiences with Leela also reminded me to pay attention to messages that come from soul friends like her. This reminder was affirmed recently by the following "thin place" story I received from Karin, a dear friend of Kate, a young mother and former Well Within board member who died a few years ago. Kate was diagnosed with a rare cancer when she was just thirty-three years old. With a fifteen-month-old son and a husband she adored, Kate was determined to live as long and as fully as she could. She was blessed to have devoted girlfriends who were committed to helping her do this. When one friend asked me for advice, I suggested they create a Sophia Group, something we had created for another Well Within friend and board member, Judy, who also lived with stage four cancer. The group met monthly to discuss their spiritual journeys with each other, including discussions regarding where God was active in their lives and other meaningful issues. During the last few years of her life, not only did these women provide loving support to Kate, but they deepened their friendships with each other; many of them are now soul friends with each other. After Kate's tragic death, the women have continued to meet regularly. Karin shared the following meant-to-be story about how their mutual friend Steph conveyed a special message from Karin's deceased father:

> Our Sophia group went and listened to Brené Brown (the bestselling author and research professor) speak last night. Afterward, my friend Steph

told me that she had a dream about my dad the other night but had no idea what it meant. She told me that in her dream my dad said to her, "Tell the girls (meaning our daughters Grace and Julia) to save a butter braid" for him. While Steph was unsure of what the dream meant, if anything, it meant a lot to me. The girls were just asked to sell butter braids (frozen pastries) as a fundraiser for gymnastics. Awesome. And it is just how my dad would say something.

Often when soul friends share meant-to-be experiences, one or both of them will get goose bumps. This often happens to me, not only with my own soul friends, but when others tell me their stories. I now pay special attention to the times when I, or the other person, have goose bumps. When they occur, it's like God is telling us to *be* especially attentive, and perhaps by doing whatever the message prompts us to *do*.

STEP II

Reflect and Discern: What Am I Called to Do and Be?

STEP 2 OF THE LIVING FULLY PROCESS INVITES US TO reflect on our meant-to-be moments and discern their meaning. Thoughtful, prayerful questions help us make sense of our life experiences. They help us discern how our relationships with others, with ourselves, and with the Divine are strengthened by meant-to-be moments. Reflecting on those relationships enables us to discern God's plan for us, and discover even more reasons to feel grateful for the life we are meant to live.

CHAPTER 4

Discerning Our Callings

To fully understand the purpose of meant-to-be moments and grow from our experiences, whether in times of grief or joy, we must practice discernment. Discernment is both an intellectual and a spiritual process of discovering our greater purpose. As we reflect on our meant-to-be moments through our human and spiritual connections, we grow personally and spiritually. Discernment enables us to discover when our inner voices and other meant-to-be moments might be guiding us toward what God calls us to be or do.

Thoughtful, prayerful discernment helps us focus. Discernment goes beyond the question of whether something is right *in general* to what is right *in particular*. The discerning person asks, *What does this meant-to-be experience tell me about myself? What does it tell me about God? Is this action consistent with who I am and what I want to become? How can these experiences lead me to a life of purpose and meaning and connectedness, both to God and to others?*

Rueben Job's book, *A Guide to Spiritual Discernment*, includes a quotation by theologian Dr. Wendy M. Wright that addresses the need for discernment when paying attention to significant experiences, such as meant-to-be moments:

> Spiritual discernment asks us to pay attention. We need to attend to both what goes on around us and within us. Ideally, this attentiveness goes on much of the time, a sort of low level, constant spiritual shifting of the data of our experience. But there are times when discernment becomes much more focused, when a crossroad is reached or a choice called for. At times like these the cumulative wisdom of tradition tells us to pay attention on many levels: to consult scripture, to seek the advice of trusted advisors, to heed the collective sense of the faithful, to read widely and deeply the best ancient and contemporary thinking, to pray, to attend to the prick of conscience and to the yearnings and dreamings of our hearts, to watch, to wait, to listen.

Discernment Techniques

Reflection and discernment require a peaceful setting. Taking a solitary walk or simply turning off the radio in the car provides rich opportunities for God's voice to be heard. For extroverts like me, conversations with others—a mentor or spiritual director, for instance—are tremendously beneficial for sharing wisdom and insight. A spiritual director, according to Margaret Guenther in *Holy Listening*, helps "connect the individual's story to *the* story and thereby helps the directee to recognize and discern the action of the Holy Spirit in his or her life."

One of the most effective discernment techniques, called the "Examen," enables us to reflect upon our day and discover God's presence in it. The Examen is a technique described by Ignatius of Loyola, founder of the Jesuit order of priests, in his book, *The Spiritual Exercises*. It is a reflective practice that can be adapted and used by people of various faith traditions to discover where God is active in our lives. Ignatian spirituality is rooted in the belief that God is active, personal, and present to all of us and that "God is found in all things." For this reason, I believe the Examen is one of the best ways to help discern God's presence and guide our response to what we have experienced, if appropriate, including meant-to-be moments.

In his excellent book, *The Jesuit Guide to (Almost) Everything: A Spirituality for Real Life*, Fr. James Martin, SJ, describes several versions of the Examen. He concludes his discussion with his own "Examen in Five Easy Steps:"

Before beginning, as in all prayer, remind yourself that you are in God's presence and ask God to help you with your prayer.

1. Gratitude: Recall anything from the day for which you are especially grateful and give thanks.
2. Review: Recall the events of the day, from start to finish, noticing where you felt God's presence

and where you accepted or turned away from any invitations to grow in love.

3. Sorrow: Recall any actions for which you are sorry.

4. Forgiveness: Ask for God's forgiveness. Decide whether you want to reconcile with anyone you have hurt.

5. Grace: Ask God for the grace you need for the next day and an ability to see God's presence more clearly.

A simple variation of this centuries-old Christian practice of daily meditation and prayer consists of asking two brief but profound questions at the end of each day:

For what moment today am I most grateful?

For what moment today am I least grateful?

By acknowledging negative as well as positive events, we uncover aspects of life that are either draining or enhancing. By naming these moments, whether with others or alone, we identify areas where God is calling us including in meant-to-be moments.

As Father Matt Linn, coauthor of *Sleeping with Bread*, explains:

When I discover something I am not grateful for, I name it, feel it, and appreciate that I am not denying it and [that] God is with me in it. Healing occurs to the degree I welcome all my feelings and let myself be loved in them. In this way, I honestly acknowledge pain and I take in love. Then I can usually fall asleep with a grateful heart.

Linn, a Jesuit priest, observes that "insignificant moments when looked at each day become significant because they form a pattern that often points the way to how God wants to give us more life.... [It] makes us aware of moments that at first seem insignificant, but ultimately can give direction to our lives."

In my case, when deciding what to do about my career as a marketing and sales professional, I was most grateful for the life-giving times of conversation and hands-on volunteer work I did, and least grateful for the demands placed on me by a career I no longer cared about. Discernment helped me notice and discover the meaning of the meant-to-be moments that guided me towards obtaining a master's degree in theology and later, opening Well Within. I was fortunate to be in a position where our family could get by without my salary. Most people can't just quit their jobs, but this process helps anyone identify the aspects of a new job that would be more fulfilling. Or if someone chose to stay in their current position, then the examen can help them chose ways to enjoy their free time more, including spending more time with family and friends and weaving in meaningful volunteer work, such as coaching, joining a board of directors, or serving meals at a homeless shelter.

In addition to helping us discover where God is active in our daily lives, discernment also enables us to determine the source of a message, voice, or intuitive feelings we notice. Discernment helps answer the question, "Is this experience from God, our own imagination, or some other source, possibly an evil one?"

Discernment helps us distinguish between good and evil. This is especially important when we believe the source of any messages we or others "hear" is from God. Sadly, some of the most destructive acts of mankind have been committed by non-discerning individuals or groups who claim to be carrying out "God's will." One easy and effective discernment technique for determining if an experience is from God is found in scripture:

But the fruit of the Spirit is love, joy, peace, forbearance, kindness, goodness, faithfulness, gentleness and self-control. (Galatians 5:22-23, NIV)

So if an experience or idea results in fear, hatred, destruction or harm to others, it most likely is not from God. Imagine what the world would be like if our actions were all motivated by the "fruits of the spirit!"

Discernment also is helpful when we are asked to choose between equal goods, such as deciding between two job offers or other opportunities that enable us to use our skills or other gifts.

For these types of situations, I like to combine aspects of St. Ignatius's Spiritual Exercises with the daily practices from the Rule of St. Benedict, used in the Benedictine tradition.

1. Listen, as Norene Vest says in *No Moment Too Small*, with the "ear of one's heart" to what God is saying to you. To do this, create a period of

silence and solitude every day. Make time for spiritual reading, including Scripture, as well as conversation with God. When you reflect upon the purpose of your life, what do you "hear?" How is God calling you to become a channel of love? Realize that "every encounter, every incident during the day is grist for the mill of the ongoing God-human communication. No activity is too small or too unimportant to mediate the holy."

2. Become indifferent to the issue or situation you are discerning. Do not be too attached to the outcome, for God may be calling you to something that is outside your comfort zone. Is there fear attached to the issue at hand? If so, examine the fear and see if there is a way through it. Ask for God's help when fear is present, especially when it might be preventing you from performing a loving act toward others. If you are not in actual danger, recognize that fear can be a sign that you are heading in the right direction—do not let it stop you from doing God's work.

3. When deciding between two "goods," identify the pros and cons of the issue. Write them down. Then pray over them. Seek counsel from a soul friend or spiritual director who knows your gifts and talents. Does the issue present an opportunity to use your gifts? Which option offers the better opportunity to be a channel of God's love?

4. After you decide what to do, confirm that it was the right decision. As noted earlier, one of the best tests is by the "fruits" of the effort: Does living it out produce positive results during the beginning, middle, and end of the experience? Use the daily Examen both to help make your decision and affirm it afterward. A journal can help with this process. If you are discerning a spiritual experience, how is the encounter consistent with the message of Scripture that portrays God as One who loves us unconditionally?

Meals on Wheels Life Lesson

My own story below demonstrates how two conflicting feelings sent mixed signals: fear, which can be an intuitive warning about real danger, and love, the concern for others that motivates me to do good works.

My husband Dan is a wonderful role model for incorporating meaningful volunteer activities into his busy life. He has been delivering Meals on Wheels to the elderly and poor for more than twenty-five years. Occasionally, when Dan can't fulfill his weekly volunteer commitment, I have delivered lunches on his route in a high crime area of the inner city. For reasons of personal safety, I was told to always have someone accompany me, so I asked a co-worker to join me. One day, my friend cancelled at the last minute and I reluctantly made the decision to deliver the meals by myself. As I drove to the various high-rise apartment buildings on Dan's route, I was filled with fear, unreasonably perhaps, but nonetheless it felt real. As a highly intuitive person, I was afraid the fear was a premonition of something bad. But no one else was available to deliver the meals and I felt responsible for my less fortunate friends.

Asking God to be with me, I decided to trust that I would be okay and began the route. As I went from place to place, I became more afraid, especially dreading going to the last stop, a locked apartment building that was part of a housing project. The sight of several teenaged boys gathered in the parking lot didn't help, even after I chided myself for reacting as a prejudicial, judgmental, suburban do-gooder.

As I unlocked the heavy security door to enter the building, I prayed, "Just be with me here, God." As soon as I said these words, I was filled with peace. The fear disappeared. Suddenly, the words from Scripture filled my mind like a song: "Whatsoever you did for the least of my brothers, that you did unto me."

In that moment, I realized the power of fear and knew instantly where it originated from—not God! In this situation, the fear nearly prevented me from doing the good I was called to do. I know now to always examine my fears to perceive if they are reasonable. If whatever I'm afraid of isn't actually happening, I reflect upon what kind act or deed the fear is preventing me from accomplishing. If my actions could potentially help someone, then I ask God to be with me as I 'feel the fear and do it anyway,' like the adage says.

The process of frequent discernment, fostered by the practice of prayer, enables us to recognize and trust God's plan and gives us the grace to fulfill it. As Danny E. Morris and Charles M. Olsen observe in *Discerning God's Will Together:*

> The promise of spiritual discernment is this: We can know and do God's will. God offers us an up-close and personal relationship. But we come to know God in the very process of our faithfulness to God—by doing God's will as we know it. The process stops if we are unfaithful to what we have heard, what we have seen, and what we know to be God's will.

Discernment is both an intellectual and a spiritual process of discovering how God is actively involved in our lives. As we look to the stories of others, we notice how God speaks to them in the still, small voice. God providentially arranges for people to meet just when they most need each other. God asks them to respond by taking care of each other and acting as an instrument of love in the world.

CHAPTER 5

Discerning Our Relationships with Others

IN DAVID'S STORY BELOW, A BRIEF INTERACTION WITH A stranger provided perspective regarding a financial crisis that affected not only him, but also nearly everyone at the company where he worked:

> I am my company's lawyer. The company is not General Motors, General Electric, Microsoft, or any of the other established "large cap" corporations. But neither are we small. We operate in the financial services sector. We have offices worldwide. We have nearly 1,500 employees.
>
> My company's stock is publicly traded on one of the big stock exchanges. We've been successful in recent years, meeting or exceeding the Street's expectations every quarter and seeing our stock price increase accordingly. It has been a good time to be a shareholder, and I've been fortunate to be the recipient of generous stock options.

Then, a few months ago, the nightmare scenario for a publicly traded company occurred. We were approaching the end of our fiscal quarter. This particular quarter was a tough one, due mostly to some industry phenomena that adversely impacted our revenue. But we had some big potential deals that still could close in the quarter and procure revenues that would once again please Wall Street.

I came into the office early that Monday. Midmorning, the company president called from out-of-state. He had just been notified that our two top revenue producers were jumping ship without notice and going to work for a competitor. These two men were the senior executives responsible for closing the deals our company was counting on to save the quarter's financial results. As the day progressed into evening, the company's finance staff frantically revisited the revenue projections for the quarter in light of the loss of these key senior executive producers. The company reached the realization that it was going to miss its quarterly revenue and income projections by a wide margin. The very difficult decision was made to issue a press release, publicly announcing that two senior executives had resigned and the company expected to miss its revenue and earnings projections by a substantial amount.

The press release was issued before the stock market opened for trading on Tuesday. The stock exchange suspended trading the company's stock for more than an hour at the opening of the market because there were no buyers in light of the information in the press release. The price of our stock plunged by nearly 70 percent until buyers began to come forward. In the space of one hour we went from a company worth nearly $1 billion to one worth about $300 million.

Our shareholders and many others, myself included, suffered significant, in some instances, devastating, financial losses. I personally watched a major portion of my wealth literally vanish before my eyes. In an hour's time, my bundle of valuable option grants went deeply underwater.

Throughout that Monday and Tuesday, as the company's attorney, I was required to make one tough judgment call after another and to give legal counsel to the rest of management and the board of directors under the most trying and stressful of circumstances. I knew all the while that my advice could well be second-guessed at a later date by shareholder attorneys, and possibly even by the Securities and Exchange Commission.

That Tuesday evening I left the office emotionally and physically drained, exhausted from lack of sleep, and worried about the company's future, as well as my own. I was as stressed as I ever have been, or could imagine being.

I pulled into the parking lot of a local Thai

restaurant to get some food to bring home with me, still distracted and absorbed in my own problems. As I walked toward the restaurant door, a man approached me. I couldn't tell how old he was— maybe twenty-five, possibly forty-five, probably somewhere in between. He was gaunt and looked terribly ill.

The man began speaking to me. He was not very coherent. That, combined with my own distractions, caused me to understand only bits and pieces of what he said.

He had full-blown HIV/AIDS. According to his doctor, he had only a very short time to live. He needed $13, possibly for medication, possibly for a place to sleep. This man was not a practiced beggar. He was very sick, very afraid, and very alone. He frantically showed me his arms to assure me he had not contracted HIV/AIDS from needles and would not use my money for drugs.

I believed him. I gave him $20. I suppose it might seem a generous act on my part, but the truth is I routinely spilled $20 bills without much thought.

The man's eyes welled up. It was as though no one had ever done a kinder thing for him. He clearly was not expecting this generosity. He fell to his knees and took my hand to kiss it in thanks. Embarrassed, I gestured for him to rise. He thanked me again and walked away, and I proceeded to buy my takeout food.

As I drove the rest of the way home that night, I found myself strangely at peace, largely relieved of the stress and anxiety I had been experiencing only moments before. I asked myself why and have reflected on the event many times since.

The man with HIV/AIDS gave me the gift of perspective. I had suffered a significant financial reversal. The modest but successful and prestigious company I worked for was in serious trouble, which could impact me professionally and financially. I had been thrown into a situation laden with legal perils and was required to give sage counsel on myriad issues with little time to reflect or study.

But I had my health. I had people who cared for me. And I was far from destitute. I realized it was almost sinful to be discouraged, worried, or depressed when I was so blessed. This was the gift the man with AIDS gave me, for a mere $20. It could be the best money I will ever spend.

IT IS SAID THAT PEOPLE COME INTO OUR LIVES FOR A REAson, a season, or a lifetime. The "reason" can range from a simple act of kindness to putting one's own life in danger for complete strangers. Others appear in our lives for a "season," when one person benefits from another's presence for a longer period of time, perhaps throughout a serious illness or a time of intense grief. Sometimes these individuals all but disappear after the reason or season, but other times the relationship deepens and lasts a lifetime. Soul friendships, such as mine with Leela, can blossom between individuals who connect at a more spiritual level.

In my work as a spiritual and wellness counselor, I've heard countless stories of people who have appeared in one's life for a reason, a season, or a lifetime. Thoughtful, prayerful discernment leads us to ask, "What does this meant-to-be experience tell me about my connection to others?"

Even the most tragic and terrifying periods in world history include heroic people who have chosen to save the lives of those whose beliefs, religion, or ethnic background differ from their own. During the Holocaust, Oscar Schindler, aided by his wife Emilee, saved more than 1,200 of his factory workers from likely extermination by the Nazis. In Poland, even after being tortured, Irena Sendler continued to risk her life by smuggling up to 2,500 children out of the Warsaw ghetto. More recently, during the 1994 Rwanda genocide, Paul Rusesabagina used his influential connections as temporary manager of a luxury hotel to shelter 1,268 Tutsis and moderate Hutus from being slaughtered by the Interahamwe militia. These inspiring individuals teach the world how love for one's neighbor can transcend fear for one's own safety.

Most of us likely will not have the opportunity to save a person's life, much less thousands of them. But we have been and will continue to be in people's lives for one reason or another, just as individuals have shown up in ours. Sometimes the encounters are so brief, as was David's with the man with HIV/AIDS, that the person's name never becomes known, yet his or her actions or words leave a lasting imprint.

Not surprisingly, David's brief encounter caused him to feel "strangely at peace, largely relieved of the stress and anxiety" he had been experiencing only moments before.

Their encounter is an example of what theologians describe as an "I–Thou" relationship, a mutually respectful *thin place* between people where God's love is felt within the kind deeds and words given and received. In his book, *I and Thou*, Martin Buber explains the difference between "I–Thou" and "I–It" relationships. In an "I–It" relationship, we relate to something or someone as an "it" when we treat them as an object, or as some "thing" to be used to serve our own interests. In an "I–Thou" relationship, we honor others rather than use or tolerate them.

To Buber, our relationship with God, the "Eternal Thou," is the foundation for "I–Thou" relationships with all others. If a person has a genuine "I–Thou" relationship with God, he or she will have an "I–Thou" relationship with the world. Thus, when we demonstrate our concern for another, God's love is present within the relationship. We feel the "peace of God that surpasses all understanding" that Scripture promises, sometimes even in the midst of chaos and crises. To me, this feeling of peacefulness is the product of grace, God's greatest gift to us. And when we reach out to others in kindness, compassion, and love, we receive that grace.

Walt Whitman observed that the best parts of good people's lives are "the small, nameless, unremembered acts of kindness and love." The stories that follow demonstrate how individuals can appear in our lives just when we most need them and how even the briefest moments of thoughtfulness can be unforgettable.

A Small Act of Kindness

One of my favorite stories comes from Nancy, a former coworker of mine. Many years ago, we were discussing some of our favorite meant-to-be experiences. One of her most memorable ones was a small but touching act of kindness that elicits goose bumps whenever I repeat this story.

One frigid January afternoon, Nancy was leaving a local grocery store when she observed an elderly man standing near the curb that adjoined the parking lot. He didn't seem to be looking for someone to pick him up, but stood quietly without moving forward. Nancy thought about asking if he needed help, but she was in a hurry, so she continued walking quickly toward her car. Her intuition compelled her to turn back and approach the man. She did so.

She walked up to him and said, "Sir, is there anything I can do to help you?"

He smiled at her, grasped her arm, and gingerly stepped off the curb onto the icy pavement of the parking lot. As he did this, he said, "Oh thank you, my dear. I hope I can help you some day." This exchange took less than two minutes. All the man needed was the steady arm of someone who cared enough to offer it. Nancy was in the man's life for only a brief moment. Yet this event reminds us of how important it is to respond to opportunities to perform "small acts of kindness and love."

An Angel's Visit

Rhonda's ongoing struggle with weight and thoughts of suicide came to a head one dark night and led to an unexpected resolution with the appearance of a human "angel":

> I could feel my throat closing as I curled up in the corner of the couch. Lisa, my daughter, was looking at me and I could hear her words, but with every sound I was flooded with all the shame and embarrassment I have ever felt about being fat. "Mom, what are you doing?" she said. I looked down at the yogurt in one hand and the spoon in the other and my world started collapsing in on me. I could see my ever-expanding body taking up more space on the couch, the shadow of who I am hidden deep inside that shell of fat.
>
> "Honey," I said, "I've hardly eaten today and this yogurt is the most I've had all day." As I once again struggled clumsily to excuse myself, I could not even see the pain and fear in her eyes because I was so lost in my own misery.
>
> What ensued were the darkest days of my life. I retired to my bedroom to hide from the world, to contemplate the seething hatred I had for it. There was no one I hated more in the world than myself.

I pushed myself into the oversized chair with a pad of paper and a pen and spewed the most hateful, deeply resentful thoughts that I have allowed myself to utter in years.

After hours of writing letters of rage, abandonment, misunderstanding, and pure self-loathing, I gave up and fell asleep. Waking up in the morning with the same burning anger in the pit of my stomach, I begrudgingly dressed myself and made an appearance.

"Mom, what's wrong?" each of my children asked in turn.

"Nothing, I'm fine." I lied.

But I was not fooling anyone. After being married for twenty years, my husband knew to stay away when I was seething. He made small talk and left for the day to visit his family. All I wanted was to be alone, so I found ways for the kids to busy themselves, and then I skulked back up to my room. The day was New Year's Eve, a time for cherishing the past and present, and starting anew. But there was no hope in my heart and no love in my soul. And so I descended further into my suicidal depression.

Being suicidal is something I have struggled with all my life, but never more than those two days. I have heard others call it the "dark night of the soul." What I did not know at the time was that you do not have to be a religious person to have this experience. So I trudged through my grief, searching for ways to reach out. When I finally hit bottom and called the suicide hotline, I was put on hold. A young woman who sounded like she could have been Lisa's age answered the phone. I sobbed deeply and could say only that I was sorry, but I didn't know why I called and I could not talk. Hanging up the phone, I cried so hard I was sure it would never end.

Then a small, still voice said, "Go online." I picked up my computer and searched "obesity." The first site I was drawn to focused on the physical health of the obese. In the article, the author mentioned that those who are obese and active are healthier than those who are thin and sedentary. As I read these words, I could feel the armor starting to open up, so that the slightest glimmer of hope could seep in. I thought to myself, "Maybe I'm not worthless after all."

Then the next link: Overeaters Anonymous. The questions they asked on the website described me so completely that I decided I would attend a meeting on Saturday. I got up from my chair, headed down the stairs, found the community education circular, and signed up for tennis and exercise classes.

Now let's face it, as a person who suffered with weight issues all my life, it would not be the first time I turned to something outside of myself for support and community. But something was different this time. It was not coming from a place of ego, but a place of peace. I didn't question it.

I moved heavily through the next few days, buying time until my first OA meeting, doing everything I could to stay present to the moment and keep my mind off what stared back at me from the mirror every day. I refused to tell my family where I was going. My pride was large and in charge, therefore I would not reach out to them for help and support. Driving to the meeting I considered turning around several times, but that small, still voice beckoned me forward.

The room was filled with people of all ages, sizes, and backgrounds. I looked around and noticed how peaceful they looked. I listened to a woman talk about her addiction and the various addictions in her family. My mind raced. "Addiction? This is ridiculous. Food is a choice, not an addiction." But I sat there and kept listening. When she was finished, the floor was open to those who wanted to share their positive experiences of healing. Every story resonated with me, each bringing me to a new awareness of my own addiction.

Before I knew it I was introducing myself: "Hi, my name is Rhonda, and I'm here because I think I'm sick." I sobbed as I recounted an abbreviated account of my experiences over the past few days. When I finished, I don't know what the reactions of others were, but I finally started to feel some sense of peace.

The meeting ended, with no discussion of what was needed to lose weight, no discussion of the "shoulds" of a healthy body, just an invitation to keep coming back. No real clarity, just the Serenity Prayer and some literature and phone numbers of other members. But "keep coming back" was the invitation, so I took it. Over the next month and a half I started working through the steps of the program, got a sponsor, and started the work of creating a connection with Spirit. I told only a handful of people of the choice I had made to join OA. Since my "ego" was trying to lead, I still needed to keep this a secret.

I shared with my trusted mentor, Randi, the connections I was making. I'd been working with Randi for the last twenty months to uncover my passion. I had finally started making intellectual connections with God, and every so often I would experience the intense peace that comes when you are truly connected. But the connection never lasted; sooner or later my self-will would take over. I told Randi I believed I had been guided to OA because I had been looking for a community to share an experience of God. I never imagined that I would have a spiritual awakening so profound that it would change my life.

In the program I was asked to do all sorts of things that my ego would fight tooth and nail: turning the food over every day to God and my sponsor, committing to what I was going to eat for the day, submitting myself to God, allowing Him to guide my life instead of me. Submission was something I had always associated with weakness, so this was no small feat. Although I had heard from others how peaceful it is to be focused only on what is in front of you and not attached to the outcome, I didn't know what that felt like. But that small, still voice encouraged me to continue. Every day, my connection to my spirit grew stronger and stronger, preparing me for the profound awakening yet to come.

Thirty-seven days after joining OA, I was traveling to New Jersey from Detroit with a layover. It was a 6:30 a.m. flight, so I got up at 3:30 in the morning. When I arrived at the airport, I was told the flight was cancelled. At that moment I felt the channel between my spirit and myself open up. Staying focused only on what was in front of me, I made arrangements to arrive in New Jersey at 8:30 p.m. Baggage checked, boarding pass, and computer in hand, I made my way through the day, totally focused on what was in front of me. My connection to Spirit was flowing. Everything was moving along so easily I was afraid to pay too much attention, afraid that the feeling would go away. But the more I relaxed into it, the more persistent the feeling became.

By the time I arrived at the layover destination, it was 2 p.m. and I had a three-and-a-half-hour wait until the next plane. Looking for a place to rest, I ran into someone who had arrived from Detroit on the same flight. He introduced himself and asked if I would join him for a drink.

We spent three hours laughing, talking about life, family, marriage, and kids. He was a young actor, writer, and producer living between California and Michigan—and as lost in the confusion of life as I was. But within the confusion was a connection—the kind where energy flows and nothing is forced, the kind that comes in the presence of pure love—pure non-romantic, nonjudgmental love. It's the feeling you get when you meet someone and you feel you have known him or her your whole life. It's an experience of comfort and ease, as if there was no one else you were intended to be with, and nowhere else you were meant to be. In that profound connection I saw God in his eyes, and I knew at once that God had sent me an angel.

This angel helped me heal my spirit in those few hours. I could literally feel my passion for life pouring back into my body. It was as if the words he spoke flowed directly from God. There was no profound meaning, no "sermon on the mount," just clarity, peace, and understanding. And when we went our separate ways, there was no sadness, just peace.

Since that meeting, my soul has been blown wide open. Every moment has been filled with so much experience, love, energy, and life that my mantra has become, "How good can you stand it?" I now understand what it means to submit, to let go and let God. I know that God is constantly sending us guides and messengers. All that is required of us is to be open to the messages. But most importantly,

I know that I would have never been open to this
experience had I not gone through the dark nights of
my soul and the unquestioned steps of reconnecting.
No coincidences—only Divine guidance.

—RHONDA

———————

PEOPLE WHO COME INTO OUR LIVES FOR A SEASON APPEAR
when we most need their help, sometimes staying for a
specific period of time, and then quietly slipping away.
Seasonal friends can help us cope with a serious illness, a
death, or the losses and adjustments associated with transition and change.

An African Welcome

Ellen's fears about moving to South Africa were eased by
a stranger even before they boarded their plane. Her new
friend later helped her cope with the year-long "season"
when she lived thousands of miles away from her Minnesota home.

When her husband received a big promotion, Ellen was
excited for him, yet nervous about moving from her Minnesota home to South Africa. Not only was the country
far away and foreign, but also the couple's preview trip to
Johannesburg, where they would be living, was frightening.
There was barbed wire everywhere and houses behind fif-
teen-foot-high walls topped with high-voltage wire. Up to
fifty murders a day were reported there.

Ellen was so apprehensive that she seriously considered separating from her husband, letting him move to South Africa on his own while she and their two daughters stayed behind. Until the day of the flight, she was still trying to decide whether to get on the plane. She finally resolved to support her husband. But Ellen was still afraid about her future, and once the family had checked in for their transcontinental flight in New York, there was no turning back.

They headed for the airline lounge, helped themselves to complimentary snacks, and looked for a place to sit. There were two rooms in the lounge, one packed and the other empty except for a man holding a screaming baby. Reluctantly, Ellen and her family sat in the second room.

A moment later, a young woman—obviously the baby's mother—came in. "Hello, Cindy!" she called out in a thick South African accent. The baby beamed and stopped crying. Now happy, the baby crawled across the lounge and grabbed a fistful of crackers from the plates of Ellen's daughters on the coffee table in front of them. The baby's mother smiled but said nothing to correct or apologize for the baby's actions. "How rude!" Ellen thought. "What kind of a mother lets her baby grab food off a stranger's plate?"

Louise, the mother, then began chatting with Ellen and her family, asking why they were visiting South Africa, where they were coming from, what they thought of South Africa from their earlier visit. Ellen and Louise discovered they had a lot in common. Word had spread quickly throughout Johannesburg's close-knit Jewish community that an American Jewish family—Ellen's family—was coming to town. Louise then asked if she could introduce Ellen to all her Jewish friends. She offered more kind gestures: Could she take Ellen on a "Best of Jewish Johannesburg" tour to show her where to get the best bagels, where to buy school uniforms for the school her daughters were attending, where to find Kosher foods, and how to recognize the Kosher coding on packages? Could she connect their family with a maid?

Ellen was astonished by this outburst of concern from someone she had only just met. While their husbands were engaged in a conversation of their own, and Ellen's daughters played with the baby, the two women visited for the entire fourteen-hour flight and never ran out of things to share. Louise and Ellen became fast friends, with Louise answering all of Ellen's questions at the end of each day. "Louise was a Godsend," Ellen says. "She not only helped me get over my many fears, but she added love and richness to my entire family's lives. Louise was literally the answer to my prayers."

Ellen was the answer to Louise's prayers as well. Louise loved America and everything American. She had lived in New York for two years as a young adult and hated to return to the violence of her own country. Ellen's friendship gave Louise strength and Louise gave Ellen strength. And although Ellen and her family returned to Minnesota after her husband's assignment, her friendship with Louise continues to this day, long distance.

A Tuscan Friendship

Carmela Tursi Hobbins' doubts about a business venture in Tuscany finally melted away once she accepted it was meant to be. When she responded to the synchronicity in her life, she found an exciting way to share her passion and talent for Italian cooking. She also found not only a business partner but also a soul friend.

Carmela's experience began after several friends and clients suggested that she read an article in *Minneapolis– St. Paul Magazine* about Doug Haynes and Doris Fortino, a Twin Cities couple who transformed a rundown *villa rustica* into a gracious Tuscan villa after one of Doris's Italian cousins encouraged them to buy the centuries-old estate.

Carmela's friends and clients encouraged her to offer tours, including cooking classes, to Italy. It was a logical next step for a gifted Italian cooking instructor and cookbook author. The idea of taking groups to her ancestral homeland and housing them at Doris's villa intrigued her. But Carmela was hesitant. Then she met a man who knew Doris, Dick H., through his daughter Terry, who is Carmela's neighbor and friend. Coincidently—or not—Carmela ran into Terry and Dick at a local café and joined them for breakfast at Terry's invitation. After learning about Carmela's culinary business, Dick said, "You should get in touch with Doris. She's trying to figure out how to make a living there." He added, "You and she are like two peas in a pod."

Carmela believes things can happen for a reason, so she paid attention to Dick's words, especially since she already was contemplating contacting Doris. Yet Carmela still resisted making the connection. As the weeks passed by, she talked herself out of it: *Why should Doris want to talk to me, a total stranger? This won't work out anyway, so why bother?*

About six weeks later, a blizzard blasted the Twin Cities. Snowed in with nothing to do, Carmela finally decided to send an email to Doris. She explained how a series of coincidences and encouragement from others, including Dick H., prompted her message. She told her about her dream of escorting tours to Tuscany and how doing so might benefit both of them.

Doris responded the next day, saying that she would love to help Carmela bring groups to her villa in Tuscany. The women emailed back and forth for several weeks. Airfares to Italy at that time weren't too expensive, and Carmela had clients who were interested in making the trip, yet she still resisted the opportunity. Previous doubts paralyzed her again and she apologetically explained to Doris that she had decided to put any further discussion on the back burner. Doris said she understood Carmela's hesitation about starting a business venture with someone she had never met, and taking groups to a part of Italy where she had never been.

But soon Carmela received another nudge at a holiday party at Terry's home. Carmela and her husband, Bob, were seated next to another neighbor, who spontaneously invited them to join her and her husband on an upcoming vacation to Italy. Their destination was a short drive from Doris's villa. To Carmela, it was no accident, and this time she accepted.

A few weeks later, Carmela and Bob visited Doris and

Doug at their Tuscan home. Doris warmly welcomed the couple with a hug and explained that a storm had caused their electricity to go out. Entering the candlelit villa, Carmela and Bob were greeted by a roaring fire and the aroma of a gourmet meal Doris had prepared on her gas stove.

During their stay, Carmela learned that she and Doris share many things in common: Both had parents who were born in Italy, both are only daughters, and both love honoring their Italian traditions, especially cooking. Both talk with their hands, can finish each other's sentences, and they even look alike. "Most importantly," Carmela says, "our husbands are not Italian, but they understand how passionate Doris and I are regarding our heritage and are patient with us. They encourage and support us fully, enabling us to achieve our dreams."

Carmela's serendipitous partnership with Doris has exceeded all her expectations. She scheduled her first culinary tour a few months after they met. The group continues to gather socially and now call themselves "The First Timers." As for Carmela and Doris, they are now "more like sisters" than business partners. Carmela says the synchronistic events leading to her relationship with Doris were "a God-thing." Not only has she created new opportunities in her professional life, but Doris has also become the sister she never had.

MANY STUDIES SHOW HOW STRONG SOCIAL NETWORKS THAT include good friends help us live longer and more fully. *Wall Street Journal* columnist Tara Parker-Pope reported on several studies that prove the point, including a 2006 study of nearly three thousand nurses with breast cancer, which found that women without close friends were four times more likely to die from the disease than women with ten or more friends.

As Dean Ornish, MD, has observed, "Nothing has a greater impact on whether you get sick and how fast you recover than love and intimacy." At Well Within, I've seen many women with stage four cancer live full and happy lives for several years beyond what doctors said might be their life expectancy, by sharing their deepest thoughts, feelings, and fears with friends they've made in our support groups.

Soul Friendships

Sometimes, a seasonal relationship evolves into a soul friendship. In the ancient Celtic world of northern England, Cornwall, Scotland, Wales, Brittany, and particularly in Ireland, a soul friend—called an *anam cara*—was akin to a therapist or spiritual director. Pagan druids and druidesses were the teachers, mentors, reconcilers, and spiritual leaders—the *anam caras* within their communities. The Celts, who had a great love of triads, claimed that every soul friendship consists of more than two people. A soul friendship is a sacred triangle of two people and the God who brought them together.

Soul friendships were an important aspect of living fully for the pre-Christian Celts. According to theologian Edward Sellner:

Wherever they went, the Celts brought with them a certain Celtic perception of the world: a belief in the spiritual dimension of all creation, a sense of kinship with the earth, a strong intuition which they called "second sight," a loyalty to family and tribe, and a valuing of friendship ties...and an appreciation of good stories.

When Christianity arrived in Ireland, its leaders appreciated the importance of these relationships. Soul friendships continued to flourish within the monasteries often built in the oak groves where the ancient Celts once worshipped.

In today's world, soul friendships involve a mutual relationship that offers all the benefits and characteristics of any good friendship, plus the added depth that comes from discussing one's spiritual journey with another person.

According to Sellner and others, some of the spiritual dimensions that exist within soul friendships include a sense of recognition when the friends first meet, a respect for each other's religious and spiritual beliefs, and a telepathic connection that cannot be diminished by time apart, age, distance, or even death itself.

A Soul Friendship with Judy

The best way I know to describe a soul friendship is to tell you about my friendship with Judy.

In early 2001, when I was volunteering at a nonprofit healing center that was the precursor of Well Within, several people asked if I knew Judy; I'm not sure why they assumed I did. When I finally did meet her at a fundraising event for the high school our children attended, she said others had similarly asked if she knew me. I don't remember what else we discussed that evening, but I do remember the feeling I had in meeting her. It was as though I had just reconnected with a longtime friend. Because this feeling often predicts a soul friendship, I knew intuitively that she and I would become close. But I also wondered how this could happen because I had heard she had been told she had less than two years to live.

Like me, Judy had been diagnosed with breast cancer. Despite aggressive treatment, her cancer recurred twice. In addition to chemotherapy, she used healing touch, acupuncture, massage, and other integrative therapies to alleviate the side effects of her illness. She was determined to enjoy life for as long as possible.

Not long after we met, Judy joined a nine-week support group I was co-facilitating on ways of coping with compromised health and other crises. As so often happens within the confidential environment of these groups, the members became close. When we no longer had a specific curriculum to follow, we decided to meet bimonthly as a Sophia Group: women seeking wisdom and spiritual growth. Our gatherings as a Sophia Group began with a prayer, reading, or song selected by a member. At one meeting, I played "You Raise Me Up," a song I first heard at a retreat center in Ireland. Judy loved it so much that I insisted she keep the CD. For Judy, the song became a prayer. She, like the Celtic *anam caras,* considered God to be her ultimate soul friend—the One who raised her up.

As Judy's journey with cancer progressed—she refused to call it a "battle"—our spiritual discussions evolved into a soul friendship. I was no longer her support-group facilitator but a good friend with whom she openly shared her thoughts and feelings, her hopes and dreams, as well as her fears. After I'd provide a healing touch session at her home, she'd send me a thank you note for my presence in her life. I often thanked her for teaching me how to cope with a life-threatening illness with courage, dignity, and grace. She dealt with fear, for example, by setting an intention—in this case, to live until her daughter's wedding several months away—then praying for it to occur. Judy also asked for the strength to deal with whatever did happen, which enabled her to cope with the times when she didn't get exactly what she wanted. Her strong faith, which we frequently discussed, reassured her that she would be present in spirit, if not physically.

Judy encouraged me to share my dreams and stories with her as well. It was important for her not only to tell her own story, but to listen and offer encouragement to others. And because she was also a good friend of Pat Walsh, my co-facilitator of the support group, Judy encouraged both of us to pursue our joint dream: opening a nonprofit wellness resource center in place of the one that had hosted our group but recently closed. It took us nearly two years to do it, but the Sophia Group went right on meeting—at Judy's home. When Well Within finally did open, in July 2004, Judy and her husband, John, both joined our board.

Judy also was one of my biggest cheerleaders as I struggled with writing my first book. Her positive feedback on my manuscript motivated me to complete *Thin Places*. She said the stories provided hope that her spiritual presence would be felt by her loved ones after she was gone. She encouraged them to watch for signs, like more of the heart-shaped stones she collected in jars around her home, which would show that she was still with them.

I invariably felt uplifted after spending time with Judy. After listening and sharing our stories through tears and laughter, we could feel God's grace in our midst. This grace was manifested in peacefulness, wisdom, compassion, love, and joy—the "fruits of the spirit" that Scripture says helps us discern God's presence.

Soul friends often share a telepathic connection, and this happened several times with Judy. Two weeks before she died, when I called to see how she was doing, Judy said she was "just thinking about me" and invited me to her home. When I arrived, Leela, whom I mentioned earlier, was there, having just finished one of her weekly healing sessions. Judy insisted the Leela and I stay for lunch. We had a delightful time together, and I remember feeling so grateful to God for bringing these special women into my life.

The final time my intuitive feelings encouraged me to stop by Judy's house I almost ignored it. I had seen her the previous day and I could tell she didn't have long to live, so I hesitated, assuming this was her time to be with family and other close friends. But the feeling persisted until I could no longer ignore it. Earlier that day, I had picked up a preliminary copy of the cover of *Thin Places*. I decided to show it to Judy and thank her again for encouraging me to finish the book.

When I arrived, Judy was curled up on her bed. She was weak but reached up with both arms to embrace me, as she always did. She was thrilled with the *Thin Places* cover and patted the open space beside her. I crawled onto the bed but we did not talk long. She said she was ready for whatever lay ahead, but worried about how John and her daughters would cope when she was gone. "But at least I made it to Sarah's wedding!" she said with a smile. She did more than that: She stood during the photos and happily visited with family and friends at the reception, knowing it would be the last time she would see most of them.

I'm so glad I listened to the inner message that prompted me to have one last conversation with my friend. By the next day, she was unable to talk, drifting in and out of consciousness. Four days later, John called to say that Judy was actively dying. I rushed to their home to say a final goodbye. He had put a hospital bed in the middle of their living room to enable family and friends to gather around her. In her final hours, she was surrounded by people telling her how much they loved her, thanking her for being such an important part of their lives, gently placing hands on her head and praying for her. It was a profoundly sacred scene.

Judy's death saddened me tremendously. But over the next few years, several thin-place incidents reassured me that the spiritual connection between us remained intact. The first happened when I was walking alone along a beach in Alabama during a family vacation. I was thinking about Judy and watching for seashells in the shape of hearts, when I saw the first one, picked it up, and then saw two more. "This is too easy," I thought, so I mentally told her, "Okay, Judy, if this is really from you, then don't let me see any for a while." So I didn't for the next half hour of my walk. Then I silently said, "Okay, let's see some more of those shells." Three more appeared within five minutes. Over the years, I have found heart-shaped stones and shells—always in threes—along beaches in Hawaii, the North Shore of Lake Superior, even in South America, where they were being sold at tourist shops in Aguas Calientes, the town at the base of Machu Picchu.

Another thin place experience occurred just before a party on the day my first book was launched. I had thought of Judy that morning and wished she were there to help celebrate. Later that day, I checked messages on my home phone. The first message came after a computerized voice said, "You have had the following message for one hundred days, the maximum time allowed." I then heard my friend's familiar voice: "Hi, Mary, it's Judy. I wanted to let you know that I just finished your manuscript and I really love it."

Other incidents occurred on important days for Judy's family, comforting both them and me. One happened about a year and a half after Judy died, on the day John was to remarry. Before she died, Judy said she hoped he would find someone else. But as I pulled into a parking spot, I wondered how she felt about this event. As if to answer me, "You Raise Me Up," the song she loved so much, began playing on the radio. Tears rolled down my cheeks as

I heard her voice in my head: "Mary, I'm so happy for John, so incredibly happy. You must tell him." At that, the tears flowed even harder: "Okay, Judy, I will."

John's eyes misted as he thanked me for telling him. "I hoped Judy would be happy for me. Now I know she really is."

Another incident occurred when Judy's second daughter, Mary, was getting married. The day before the ceremony, I had my wedding gift for her wrapped at the store. As I waited, I checked messages on my home phone, using my cell phone. Once again, a saved voice message from Judy spoke to me, thanking me for a healing touch treatment earlier that day. Like me, Mary interpreted the incident as Judy's way of showing her continued presence in their lives.

I have no doubt that Judy was in my life for a reason. Coming out of the corporate world, I had very little experience working with people with life-threatening illnesses. Judy helped build my confidence in doing this work. She taught me how to live in the present moment, and how to find the good within every situation. From her, I received the gift of soul friendship. But most of all, she taught me the importance of trusting in God, especially during the most challenging times, including at the end of our lives.

LIKE THE ANCIENT CELTS, I BELIEVE SOUL FRIENDS, INCLUDING Judy, help bring us closer to God. I interpret the spiritual dimensions, including thin place experiences and other fruits of the spirit, as indications of God's presence within the sacred triangle of soul friendships. Like the soul friend who listens intently, offers sage advice, helps us identify and use our gifts, and helps us grow spiritually, God loves us unconditionally.

Christian author C.S. Lewis did not think it is an accident that people end up in each other's lives:

> In friendship, we think we have chosen our peers. In reality, a few years difference in the dates of our births, a few more miles between certain houses, the choice of one university instead of another . . . any of these chances might have kept us apart. But for a Christian, there are, strictly speaking, no chances. A secret Master of Ceremonies has been at work.

These stories, from non-Christians as well as Christians, demonstrate that it is not any one particular faith community for whom there are "no chances." Reflecting and discerning the meaning and impact of meant-to-be moments often results in a greater awareness of how God works in our lives for our benefit and to help others.

Reflection and discernment also prompt requests or prayers for wisdom that become a dialogue with the Divine that invites us into the *ultimate* soul friendship.

CHAPTER 6

Discerning Our Relationship With the Divine

Some meant-to-be moments are miraculous, with no apparent explanation for them except for the possibility of Divine intervention. These inexplicable events are transformational, not only for the person who had the experience, but for many of us who hear about them and realize there must be a God who enabled whatever occurred.

A Miracle in Greece

The meaning of meant-to-be coincidences became clear for Steve after his twin brother Tom experienced a miraculous intervention that saved his life. Both events affirmed the men's faith, enabling them to deepen their relationship with God.

Steve, who was raised Greek Orthodox, lives on the East Coast but often travels to Minneapolis on business. One evening, when he was dining at his favorite Greek restaurant in Minneapolis, he noticed a waitress staring curiously at him. He struck up a conversation with her and soon learned she was from a small town in northern Greece—the same area, he told her, where his identical twin brother was studying Greek Orthodox icons on a Fulbright scholarship. The waitress smiled and said, "I know. I recognized you as Tom's brother as soon as you walked in." She had just returned from Greece on an extended visit to her hometown and had met Tom at a local bookstore.

Steve believes things happen for a reason. A few weeks later he learned the likely reason for meeting the waitress when he received word of a near-tragedy suffered by his brother, who was still in Greece.

Tom had been walking down a rugged, seldom used path near a Byzantine monastery on Mount Athos when the path, formed by a long-gone waterfall, crumbled. It was May 30, the feast of the Ascension. He plunged about one hundred and fifty feet, halfway down a cliff face of the mountain. Tom was knocked unconscious; he is not sure for how long. "When I came to," he says, "I saw blood everywhere. I saw bones sticking out of my left arm. One of my legs was caught in a thorny bush that grew on a ledge and the other leg hung over the edge of the cliff."

Tom realized he was perilously close to the cliff's edge. As he groggily tried to determine what had prevented him from falling further, he became aware that his "body was being cradled by a crimson-colored shoulder, with an arm wrapped around my midsection. It was definitely that of a woman." He recognized the colors from his study of icons; in the Greek Orthodox religion, icons traditionally portray the Virgin Mary wearing crimson or maroon clothing. Tom closed his eyes. When he reopened them, he was surrounded by a brilliant white light that vanished after a moment.

Stranded, severely injured, and unable to move, he could see the tops of trees below him and began considering his options. After some time, he began to despair. He was tempted to throw himself off the edge of the cliff and put an end to his suffering, believing no one would ever find him in this remote place. But a booming voice inside him said, "Like hell you will! Who do you think you are that you are so special you can decide your own fate?" Inspired, he found the strength to crawl back from the ledge, away from the cliff. "An incredible survival instinct kicked in," he recalls. "I wasn't even in control of it."

To satisfy his hunger, he ate toothpaste, moss, and a handful of chickpeas and raisins, rationed to four to five per "meal." To quench his thirst, he squeezed mud between his fingers, and then licked his hands. The raisins expanded from the morning dew and provided a tiny amount of additional liquid. He conserved his energy by yelling only when he heard a boat arriving or departing from the nearby coastline. During the long night, his mind "filled with the faces of everyone I had ever loved." He visualized those people handing him cans of Coke and food, and he imagined himself thanking them for helping him survive.

On the morning of the second day, Tom saw a swatch of fabric clinging to the branch of a small tree above his head. He knew that others had died on Mount Athos, and he presumed the cloth was a remnant from another person's fall. It became a reverential reminder for Tom to be grateful for being alive.

Finally, on the third day, Tom's cries for help were heard. In dramatic fashion, Greek villagers, monks, and an experienced rescue team brought him to safety. His doctors told him it was a miracle he had no infections from his injuries, which included a broken collarbone and cervical vertebrae, a partially dislocated shoulder, and bruised ribs. The doctors also were amazed that his left arm, despite being shattered in thirty-two places, showed no nerve damage or cut arteries.

When Steve heard of Tom's accident and the severity of his injuries, he was concerned about the quality of medical care Tom was receiving in this remote part of Greece. He contacted the waitress, who referred him to a wonderful local doctor who helped his brother recover. But his recuperation was slow. Several months after the accident, Tom was still in pain and undergoing extensive physical therapy.

By most people's standards, his accident and injuries would be a tragedy. But for Tom, it was life affirming. At the time of the accident, Tom had been in a self-described "spiritual abyss," depressed and alienated from God. During his recuperation, he experienced an explosion of personal and spiritual growth. "I believe this accident was supposed to happen, almost like a test of what's important in my life," he says. "Faith, hope, and charity—these are most important. I learned about the power of God's love, which is infinite, never-ending." Tom now lives a simpler life, one day at a time, not worrying about things he cannot change.

Tom experienced another strange coincidence related to his accident. As it turns out, he is an artist as well as a student of religious art. While recuperating, he came across a series of twenty-two paintings he had drawn months before the accident, which he had titled "Out of Darkness." The paintings showed, in progression, a silhouetted person falling off the edge of something, and then sprawling on a platform. The person goes from a dark to light form as the scene progresses. When Tom had painted these scenes, his intention was to portray life as a pregame warm-up, an interim step toward the end, which is death and then eternal life. In reviewing these paintings after the accident, however, he was stunned by the striking similarity to his accident. He realized that God had been trying to get his attention and that he had not been listening. This coincidence, and his resulting insight that he had drifted away from God, served as the catalyst for his tremendous spiritual growth after the accident.

Since that transformational event many years ago, Tom says he has developed much more compassion, choosing to align himself with others who are suffering around the world. He now knows he is never alone; God is always with him. He counsels that we all must listen to our inner voices. When it really is from God, "you just know it," he says.

———————

RAYMOND MOODY DRAMATICALLY REVEALED AN AWARENESS of what occurs at or near the time of death back in 1975, in his book *Life After Life*. Moody coined the term "near-death experience" to describe the remarkably similar events— such as seeing a brilliant white light—that often occur when someone is thought to have died and yet survives.

Like so many others who have had brushes with death,

Tom was transformed by his experience on Mount Athos. "When they return [from a near-death experience], people are profoundly changed," Moody observed in a documentary based on *Life After Life*. "They are imbued with a new value structure. Their value is to seek loving relationships with fellow human beings and they have no fear of death whatsoever."

Moody summarized his own beliefs about near-death experiences in an interview with Dr. Jeffrey Mislove:

> After talking with over a thousand people who have had these experiences, and having experienced many times some of the really baffling and unusual features of these experiences, it has given me great confidence that there is a life after death. As a matter of fact, I must confess to you in all honesty, I have absolutely no doubt, on the basis of what my patients have told me, that they did get a glimpse of the beyond.

In December 1997, George Gallup observed that although 96 percent of the U.S. population believes in a higher power, over one-fourth of this group could not conceive of a loving, personal God. Mother Teresa shed light on this predicament: "The spiritual poverty of the Western world is very great. People know they need something more than money, yet they don't know what it is. What they are missing, really, is a living relationship with God."

Often the initial barrier to this relationship is one's image of God. Tom's relationship with God was restored through his encounter with the Virgin Mary and the bright light, as well as the rediscovery of the paintings that foretold his accident. He no longer felt spiritually adrift or alone. His relationship with his fellow human beings, especially those who endure suffering, was strengthened through his own suffering during and after his fall.

Tom's "glimpse of the beyond" caused a spiritual reawakening that was swift and sure.

A Spiritual Awakening

Abby's awakening took several years. When she was nine years old, her mother died unexpectedly of a heart attack. Abby was devastated. She was angry with God for years, and because she had no faith in God, she could not and did not turn to God for comfort. Nor did she understand, until years later, the meant-to-be moments that seemed to occur before and after her mother's death.

Before she died, Abby's mother made each of her children attend the funeral of a stranger, as if trying to prepare them for her own death. She showed a renewed desire to enjoy life and live in the moment, such as taking up the sport of golf. She was happy and at peace. After her mother died, Abby dreamt about her, but she wasn't comforted by the dreams. She didn't feel a spiritual connection to her mother or to God through them.

Several years passed. Abby remained a nonbeliever, even after falling in love with a devout Christian who was active in his Lutheran church. Sam had had leukemia as a child but when he met Abby, his disease was in remission.

Eventually, they married. Despite her doubts about God, she said a simple prayer every night with her husband: "Dear God, we trust in you. We know you are with us and will make everything all right."

Sam's leukemia returned three years into their marriage. During his illness, he drew on his deep faith, both for his own comfort as well as Abby's. He told her she should continue to trust God as they said they would in their simple prayer each night.

Sam lived nearly two years after his leukemia reoccurred. Shortly before he died, Abby lay next to him in bed and expressed her doubts about heaven. She wanted to believe there was something beyond this life. "If you see my mother there," she asked Sam, "will you please send me some sort of sign?" Sam, like many others who are near death, had dreams and visions of his deceased loved ones, including his grandfather. Remembering the puzzling vision of a woman he did not know, Sam answered his wife, "I think I already have seen your mother."

On the day Sam died, Abby left his hospital room, too distraught to be there at the moment of his death. But when two of her friends encouraged her to return to his bedside, she did. As soon as she walked back into the room, Abby says, she felt better than she ever had in her entire life. "It was as though Sam had jumped into my heart." She sensed that, although he was barely alive, his soul had separated from his body. "The feeling was like the closeness you want with someone but can never achieve because of barriers created by the body and the mind," she says. "I felt a pure sense of love. I had no doubt he was fine and at peace.

Sam could go anywhere; his body no longer trapped him. It was an incredible feeling. There are no words to convey the emotions I felt at that moment. Since then, I have had absolute confidence that God is real."

For Abby, a logical and analytical person, this powerful meant-to-be moment demonstrated another dimension to life that she had resisted since her mother's death, a spiritual, God-centered dimension. She could feel it, and found this knowledge to be beautiful and comforting. Abby now feels connected to a higher power. She is not a churchgoer, but considers herself a spiritual person. Her belief system was fundamentally altered by the intense experiences surrounding Sam's death. It would seem that, in a subtle way, through her prayers with her devout husband, Abby had opened her heart to receive God's love and grace. The result was a joy and peace that was entirely lacking when her mother died.

A Child's Loss, a Mother's Faith

How do parents arrive at a place of faith at the most tragic time of their lives? For Theresa and Donn Zimanski, they "didn't know how close Jesus could be" until going through the heartbreaking experience of losing their twelve-year-old son.

On March 12, 2005, in one of the last journal entries on her son's CaringBridge website, Theresa wrote, "At 4:15 p.m., Michael's eyes saw a perfect place; he took his last breath, and went home. Although we are deeply saddened by the loss of our dear sweet Michael, we find comfort knowing that he is now running on streets of gold. This is not the end, just the beginning of his glory."

Even his final moments were filled with grace: "Hope has turned to acceptance for what has come for Michael. We are faithfully confident that God is with us every second, not only holding Michael in the palm of His hand, but pouring out his love and grace on each one of us."

Michael had been born with kidneys not designed to last past puberty. When diagnosed on Dec. 16, 1999, he was just 6 years old. When his devastated parents cried out, "Why our boy?" Theresa heard an inner response: "This isn't your little boy. I gave you that little boy." From that moment on, she knew "he was not mine. I had to give him back."

Other times, she heard words that guided her, coming as thoughts she knew she did not generate. When she heard the command, "I need you to rest," she heeded it, enabling her to maintain her strength when she most needed it.

Michael received the last of three kidney transplants on Aug. 30, 2004. During these difficult years, the couple felt God's presence in certain people who surrounded them, including the youth minister from their Lutheran church. Theresa believes it was God who led her to a Bible study group of women in the spring of 2006. The women welcomed her warmly at a time when she felt disconnected from most other people. There she found comfort and wisdom while studying Scripture, believing "Scripture tells us what we need to know."

Trying to understand why Michael was ill, his mother asked for answers, for herself and for her young son. One night, she had a dream. In it, God said to her, "I needed the bravest, strongest warrior to do a really big job." Michael was the warrior to whom he said, "Put on your armor." Michael came to the front and said, "I could do that." The dream brought her great comfort. She did not understand fully God's plan, but the dream affirmed her belief that God had not abandoned her family during this crisis.

Toward the end of her son's life, Theresa heard more specific messages that helped her cope. Sometimes the messages were prophetically personal, like the simple advice, "You need a haircut." She didn't know it at the time, but the funeral for her son would be in less than a week. And she did need a haircut. Just before Michael died, she heard, "Are you ready for this?" She responded with "I think I am ready." Then she was told, "It's going to be a really hard day today." And it was, heartbreakingly so.

After her son's death, Theresa had an understandably difficult time giving away many of Michael's possessions. Unsure about whether she could bear to part with any item he had once touched, she heard, "Yes, you can." Then, "Trust me, I will meet you there."

Michael's illness and death brought Teresa, Donn, and their daughter, Jessica, closer than ever before. It also brought the family closer to God. Buoyed by the power of the intercessory prayers of family, friends, and even strangers, they eventually concluded that Michael indeed was healed, but "it just wasn't *here*."

Their renewed faith helped Teresa when she was diagnosed with breast cancer a few years later. Her recovery did not come easily. She had several surgeries, including a complete hysterectomy, gall bladder removal, and a double mastectomy with two failed reconstructions of her breasts.

Despite her grief and her own poor health, Theresa eventually returned to work. After all that has occurred, her faith in God remains strong, in part because of the loving relationship she has with the Divine, whose presence has been manifested so profoundly in the meant-to-be moments in her life.

A Glorious Sunrise

Despite the heartbreaking experience of losing their daughter Katie, her parents felt the continuing presence of God's comfort and mercy for their family in a sunrise of unparalleled beauty:

> At our routine twenty-week ultrasound, my husband and I learned that our baby (our third child) no longer had a heartbeat. Having had no symptoms of anything going wrong with the pregnancy, the news was especially devastating. My grief turned into fear when I learned that the safest way to deliver my baby's body would be through labor inducement. How could I go through labor and delivery knowing there would be no healthy baby as the reward? My fears increased when my doctor warned that this type of labor usually takes much longer than a full-term labor/delivery process. My husband and I also were filled with fear as we

thought about holding our dead baby. We begged our family and friends for prayers and checked into the hospital.

The story of Katherine's "birth," which follows, had an unexpected ending and is a powerful testament of God's faithfulness, mercy, and love. We shared it at her prayer service and have told it to many others since:

It may be difficult for any of you to imagine calling the moment of Katherine's birth a gift, but as her parents, we believe that's exactly what God intended. You see, our little Kate was born at five o'clock in the morning, and we are convinced this timing was no accident. With labor induced at ten o'clock the night before, the doctor and nurses told us to expect nothing for at least twelve to sixteen hours, maybe not even for two whole days. We were prepared for a long, difficult night and an even longer, more grueling day. Yet only seven hours into the process (half the time promised by the experts) Katherine's body came into the world.

Delivery of the placenta and other routine procedures took another hour and a half or so. It was not until almost seven o'clock in the morning that we were able to hold our little girl. It was the moment we half-longed for, half-dreaded. We had fears of becoming overwhelmed with a grief that would never leave us.

At the same time that we daringly held, examined, kissed, and admired our baby, the sun was rising. Our hospital room faced east, and from our wall of windows on the fourth floor, we were able to see the bright golden sun peek its way through the scattered clouds. At first, it was an intensely bright yellow ball, slightly covered behind the breaking clouds. Then, as it rose further, there were large, glowing beams of light that dashed downward through the sky and landed right in our hospital room.

As we sat holding our child, our eyes were drawn to the beautiful sight out our window, and Katie's message to us rang loud and clear. She said, 'Mommy and Daddy, do not look for me in that tiny, fragile, cold body you hold in a blanket. Look for me here in the grand, brilliant warmth of the sun. It is here that my spirit dwells with our Father in heaven. And it is from here that I send you my peace and my love.'

While sitting with our daughter at that moment, we truly were filled with an overpowering sense of peace. The tears stopped. There were no sick feelings in our stomachs, just a calm appreciation for the moment. God had shown us his mercy and answered the many prayers sent to Him on our behalf. In those precious morning minutes, He had given us a lasting gift. He meant for us to see that perfect sunrise. And He meant for us to do so while holding Katie in our arms. What He meant for us to understand was that although we no longer have Katherine to hold and to touch, we will always have the sunrise.

We took many pictures of that sunrise out our window (none of which do it justice, of course) and, unbeknownst to us, our neighbor also noticed how the sunrise (it seemed to her) settled right over our house that morning. It moved her to take a picture of it, and later we were surprised to find that we both thought God was sending us a message of peace and love that morning. I used our neighbor's picture on our Christmas card last year to share with others the story that God is very much alive and with us, even in our darkest hours.

In the years that have passed since this life-changing event, I have been incredibly grateful for the gift of the sunrise that morning. Now, anytime I feel drawn to spend time with my daughter, I just get up early, sit at our kitchen table, and wait for the sun to rise. It is a peaceful, reverent time for me. Katherine is buried at the cemetery of my husband's hometown church, twenty-five minutes away from our home. So the sunrise has been a wonderful way for me to feel like I am visiting my daughter without even having to leave home. That has been extremely comforting.

—Christine Majeski

Deathbed Revelation

Sometimes, a true understanding God's presence doesn't reveal itself until the final moments of life.

For Angela, the faith she had professed for so many years seemed fragile. A Roman Catholic, she had been active in her church and participated fully in the rituals of her religious tradition. Her family was distraught, and somewhat surprised, at the anxiety and angst she exhibited as death approached. Surrounded by a loving family, who had done everything they could to ease her distress, they reassured her that it was okay for her to let go and "Go home to God." But Angela could not say goodbye to them. She could not let go. She was terrified and agitated. Eventually, her family could no longer bear to witness her discomfort. So they called the hospice chaplain to act, as Margaret Guenther so aptly describes in *Holy Listening: The Art of Spiritual Direction*, as a "midwife to her soul."

When the chaplain arrived at her home, Angela was still lucid and able to communicate. Despite administration of the Sacrament of Healing, she was not comforted. Acting in his role as spiritual director, the priest gently probed to discover the source of her fear. "Angela, are you afraid to die?" No, that was not it. Her faith provided hope of eternal life. He tried another approach: "What is your concept of God?" With this question, she began to cry. She described God as a paternal, authoritative figure she was terrified to face. She tearfully claimed she did not feel worthy of God's love; instead, she had lived her life feeling "never quite good enough."

The chaplain then asked about her life experiences, especially her childhood relationship with her father. Angela described herself as the daughter of an alcoholic father who was abusive, both physically and verbally. The chaplain realized that Angela's negative image of God, so entwined with the traumatic relationship she had with her father, had prevented a loving, personal relationship with the Divine.

Next, the spiritual director asked about Angela's husband. She spoke of him kindly, "Oh, he is a wonderful father. He spends a lot of time with our children; he is very affectionate and loving." With that insight, and with further questions, the priest then was able to help the woman revise her image of God. In that brief conversation, he helped Angela see God as more like the loving father she knew her husband to be. She died peacefully, an hour later, with the reassurance that she was, always had been, and forever would be unconditionally loved.

———————

THROUGH DISCERNMENT OF MEANT-TO-BE MOMENTS, OUR relationships with others, with ourselves, and with the Divine are strengthened. Reflecting upon such relationships often results in gratitude to the higher power who is so actively involved in our lives. Gratitude is one of the most important aspects of living a full and happy life.

STEP III

ASK and ACKNOWLEDGE:
Seeking Guidance and Being Grateful
for Meant-to-Be Moments

THE THIRD STEP OF THE LIVING FULLY FORMULA ENCOUR-
ages us to Ask for help when we need it, and to Acknowledge Divine Providence when we perceive it. As we become
more attentive to meant-to-be moments and their meaning,
God's actions become more evident within our daily lives.
When our prayers are answered, we realize that we are not
alone, especially during the most difficult times in our lives.
And even when we haven't *asked* for help, but *acknowledge*
its presence when it comes to us unbidden, we are express-
ing gratitude for the gifts and guidance we receive. As we
become focused on the movement of God in our lives, we
become increasingly aware that God hears and responds to
our requests and also provides invaluable help even when
we don't ask for it.

This step also invites us to ask for comfort in times of grief and wisdom to make the right choices in life. It demonstrates the importance of calling on the Divine, and perhaps a spiritual director or soul friend, for clarity and guidance as we try to understand the meaning of our experiences. Amazingly, just the simple act of asking can prompt an incident that appears to be a direct response to our request.

Finally, step three reminds us to acknowledge and be grateful for the meant-to-be times that become increasingly apparent to us. Ultimately, asking for help and acknowledging God's presence leads to a relationship with God that is based on mutual trust and love. Our prayers and expressions of gratitude thus become a dialogue with the Divine. And that dialogue is our invitation into our ultimate relationship—a soul friendship with God.

CHAPTER 7

Ask for Wisdom and Guidance

THE PROGRESSION OF HER MOTHER'S ALZHEIMER'S DISEASE was painful for Lori to watch. Sometimes she needed guidance because she simply did not know how to respond to the many difficult dilemmas posed by her mother's illness. Over time, she has learned that she needed "to surrender to the pain, be willing to ask for help, and be open to listen for the answer":

> Today, as I went to visit my mother in her new room on the lowest functioning unit of the Alzheimer's facility, I had to prepare myself for the stark differences I would notice in her surroundings. My mind equated it to ramming a car into a wall at 50 mph. I was anticipating the crash and the destruction that lay ahead.
>
> If you are ever faced with the relentless progression of Alzheimer's disease, you will find that your boat will routinely get flipped into the River of Denial. This was one of those times. Each time is always shocking and demoralizing at best. Mom

had started to wander outside, alone. Not good, especially with her uneven gait and lack of balance and direction. The move to increased care was necessary and hard for all of us.

Today, my boat was being turned over again. My body absorbed the River of Denial's cold, bitter water in the darkness of my mind, heart, and soul. As I punched in the security code to go to Mom's floor in the elevator, I could feel stabbing pains in my chest. I took a deep breath; I needed all the oxygen I could get to help me through this moment, this scheduled and necessary boat flip. As I slowly forced myself to walk down the hall, I heard my mother's voice. My gait quickened as I rushed towards her. She was angry. No, she was downright mad!

The sound of her voice led me straight to her room. I read her nameplate to the left of the door. This was it. This was my mother's new room. I just stood in the hallway outside her room and listened to the conversation. Mom was yelling. Profanity spewed from her lips, a singular and shocking statement to the changes my mother has gone through as the disease continues to overpower every facet of her personality. In the past, Mom had always been the first to shove a bar of soap in our mouths to clean up our language.

"Dorothy," I heard a female staff say in a calm, soothing voice, "Dorothy, we are here to help you. We want to get you off the bed, and into your wheelchair. It's lunchtime, Dorothy." There was a brief pause on the staff's part, but my mother kept swearing.

Another patient voice, this time a man, said, "Dorothy, we need your arms straight and knees bent. Come on, Dorothy, you can do this. We are here to help. Once your knees are bent and your arms are straight, I'm going to push the button and the machine will lift you up so we can get you into your chair."

Tears welled up in my eyes and my vision blurred. I could feel warm tears streaming down my cheeks; my nose began to run. I listened, clutching my stomach, as pain overtook my body. Poor Mom, I thought, the more disconnected her brain becomes, the more fear she feels. I stood paralyzed outside the doorway and prayed for help: "Please, dear God, help me. Help my mother. Help the staff. Tell me how I can make this better. How can I remove Mom's fear and help her feel calm and responsive? What can I do? Please, dear God, there has to be something."

I gathered my courage, prayed for my body to stop shaking, and pushed the heavy, extra wide, handicap door open. No one heard me come in. Mom was still screaming. The staff repeated their requests again.

An instant later, I heard my dad's voice as clear as a bell: "Lori, ask Mom to go water skiing." I could feel the comfort of his arm wrap around my shoulder, and I felt safe. I felt strong. I could do this.

Wait a second, I thought. Dad is dead and talking to me about taking Mom water skiing? Wow, I'm really losing it. Am I going to be Mom's next roommate? Then, *BOOM!* It hit me. I wiped the tears from my eyes and walked toward the bed where mom was sitting, legs out straight, feet off the floor. She was leaning back. There was a seatbelt-type strap around her waist that connected to a lift machine. Ropes from the machine were attached to her wrists. Her spine was about a foot off the bed. Terribly afraid, she continued to scream and yell at the staff.

"Mom," I said as I approached the end of her bed. "Mom, do you want to go water skiing?" Her head turned briskly toward me. She recognized my voice. Her face melted. A blissful calm came over her. "Of course I want to go water skiing!" she said in a strong, confident tone.

Both staff looked at me like I was nuts. I couldn't blame them. "Okay then, Mom, let's go water skiing. Knees bent, arms straight, HIT IT!" I pointed at the staff to push the button. There was a low hum from the machine, and my mother rose proudly up and off the bed with ease. The smile on her face was like a beautiful sunrise. Her eyes widened in excitement, and the staff, well, they beamed too, in awe of the whole scene. "You go, Dorothy!" the man said, and my mom winked, as she held tight to the tow rope and glided around the lake in her mind.

"Thanks, Dad. Thanks, God. We couldn't have done this without you!" I said to myself, as my heart filled with warmth and light. Thank you, I said silently again. I, too, felt safe and in control, like my mother. Once again, God rescued me from the River of Denial.

—LORI LE BAY

WHEN WE ASK FOR WHAT WE NEED, WE OFTEN RECEIVE IT. In Lori's case, after asking for guidance, she heard an inner message and immediately knew how to respond. Her story illustrates how the answer often comes creatively and, at times, via a message from someone we have loved and lost.

SEVERAL PEOPLE HAVE SHARED STORIES DEMONSTRATING how they have asked for a response from a deceased loved one, then heard an inner message or observed something that seemed to be the answer they sought. My husband—the analytical lawyer—is skeptical of these types of incidents because they aren't "logical." Yet after he and I shared a meant-to-be incident involving his father, who had died less than a year earlier, he has become more open to these experiences.

Dan and I were staying at a resort on Leech Lake in northern Minnesota and decided to go hiking in nearby Itasca State Park, where you can walk across the Mississippi River at its source. He reminisced about the last time he visited Leech Lake. When he was ten or eleven years old, Dan's family was invited to stay at the vacation home of one of his father's friends. Dan couldn't remember the man's name, nor could I, although I did remember Dan telling me about the man's kind gesture after we were first married over 40 years ago. We both remembered he was from Little Falls, but nothing more than that.

Dan said, "If only Dad were still alive right now, I'd call him up and ask him." Because I believe we can communicate with those we have loved and lost, I quickly replied, "You still can ask him even if he's not physically here."

Without hesitation, I asked my father-in-law, "What's the name of the friend who invited you to his cabin?" Immediately and simultaneously, the name popped into our heads and Dan and I both spoke it aloud: "Gordon Rosenmeier." We looked at each other and laughed. "Thanks Bob!" I said. Despite his doubts and skepticism, Dan admits it's hard *not* to believe that his father communicated the name to us at exactly the same moment.

———

ASKING FOR GUIDANCE WHEN MAKING DECISIONS OFTEN results in a direct response to our request. The following stories bear witness to that guidance.

A Life-or-Death Decision

When asked for guidance about one of the most important choices she'd ever have to make, a reassuring message from God told Ginna she would soon hear the advice she and her husband so desperately sought.

From the start, Ginna's pregnancy had been difficult.

She had been carrying twins, but sadly lost one baby at seven weeks. Not long after, an ultrasound revealed that the surviving baby's placenta might separate from the uterine wall and cause hemorrhaging, so Ginna was hospitalized for the remainder of her pregnancy. At four months, she and her husband received more bad news: another test revealed that the surviving baby was severely brain damaged.

Ginna and her husband, Tim, faced an unthinkable choice: whether to abort the pregnancy or carry the baby full term, knowing it would be severely handicapped. They prayed for guidance in making this difficult decision. One night during a particularly intense period of prayer, Ginna sensed that God was telling her, "Don't worry. I will give you your answer soon." With that assurance, she stopped worrying and was able to sleep.

The following day, Ginna received an unexpected visitor: a priest who was an old family friend. The priest was visiting someone else at the hospital and had seen Ginna's name on a patient list. Ginna sought her friend's counsel on the heartbreaking dilemma she and Tim faced. He advised her on the Catholic Church's position: It is for God alone to decide whether the baby survives. She believed this was the answer she had been promised the previous evening, and she resolved to see the difficult pregnancy through, a decision that gave her a sense of peace.

Molly was born at twenty-nine weeks. She required immediate surgery to remove a mass in her brain and to implant a shunt, requiring hospitalization for two months after her birth. Molly was, as predicted, mentally and physically handicapped, although not as severely as the doctors had thought. She has since grown into a young adult with the mind of a child and a disabled body that can barely manage to crawl.

By most standards, Molly's handicaps might be considered a tragedy that could have been avoided. But to her immediate and extended family, she has been a blessing. Her three siblings and their families adore and protect her. She loves people, and they, in turn, are drawn to her warm smile and good humor. Molly has been a source of joy and inspiration, adding a dimension to her family's life that they could not have anticipated at the time of her birth.

Ginna believes God has continued to watch over Molly. When she was 7 years old, she began complaining of a sore neck, and soon a lump appeared on the side of her neck. An infection developed and spread to the incision where the shunt had been inserted in her brain after her birth. Despite months of testing, two surgeries, and weeks in intensive care, the problem persisted.

One evening while praying for help, Ginna heard the following message: "Call your brother-in-law, Steve." Steve, a radiologist, ordered x-rays, which revealed something that had been previously missed: a tiny piece of surgical tubing left in Molly's neck during her first surgery. When Molly's surgeon removed the infected piece of tubing her neck problems vanished and have never reappeared. The bonus? Molly and her Uncle Steve have enjoyed a very special relationship ever since.

Ginna's next story also relates to Molly. When Molly was about 9 years old, Ginna attended a weekend retreat sponsored by her church. She shared with her fellow

retreatants the hard choices she faced during her pregnancy and the many blessings she and her family have
received because she and her husband had placed their
faith in God. After she returned home, her mother dropped
by for a cup of coffee. As Ginna described the weekend,
her mother commented on a photo on the kitchen counter
of Ginna and Molly. She noted how nicely the gold frame
matched the brass candlestick holder sitting next to it. At
first Ginna was confused. She knew she had placed the picture in a *silver* frame shortly before the retreat. Then she
examined the frame closely: Although the knob at the top
was still silver, the rest had changed to gold. Ginna felt as
though God was reaffirming her choices about Molly, telling her, "You are my beloved. In you, I am well pleased."

Acknowledging Meant-to-Be Guidance

Mary did not *ask* for specific help when she was making a
major decision about whether she should move to Australia
to be with a man she had only met online. As she explains,
"I am not religious, I do not attend church or follow a doctrine. But I believe in God in my own way. I do not believe
in coincidence or chance." For Mary, the "meant–to-be
incidents made me realize that if God intended for me to
move, there was no way around it." So rather than *asking*,
she paid close attention and reflected upon what was happening in her life, then *acknowledged* God's role in it. She
now believes God nudged her to say, "Yes!" to the life she
believes she was meant to live. Here's her story:

In March 2008, I had a severe allergic reaction to a prescribed drug, which caused me to have a near-death experience. I believe I died for a short time. When I was released from the hospital, I told my daughter what happened and that I was certain a life-changing experience was in the works for me.

About a month later, I met a man from Australia online. I did not consider it at the time, but my friendship with Rick became my "meant-to-be" life change. I believe this is true because of several things that occurred preceding our initial meeting. First, I struggled with the decision to move to Australia. To put it simply, I did not want to go. I was extremely scared of flying and had never gone abroad. So one day I decided to send Rick an email saying I was cutting off my friendship with him. I didn't want to leave my home, my adult daughter or my stuff! But strange things began to happen. It felt like I was being dragged by my heels to Australia.

Happy with my decision to stay in Indianapolis, I was driving home when I came to a stoplight. A man crossed the street wearing an Australian flag T-shirt! The next day, still happy with my decision to stay put, I came home and flipped on the TV. The first words I heard were, "And the Australian fauna…" It seemed I was destined to move Down Under.

When I finally made it on a flight bound for Australia, a computer glitch in Chicago stranded hundreds of people at the airport, including myself.

I was given a hotel room, but I had to stand in line for three hours to check in because there were so many of us. This flight to Australia wasn't working out. I was barely three hundred miles from Indianapolis and already things were a disaster! I decided to cash in my ticket and go back home. I was feeling relieved about my decision until I went to the gift shop to get toiletries. As I reached for a can of deodorant, I bumped into the man standing behind me. When I apologized, he replied with an Aussie accent. He was, of all things, an Australian cowboy! Of the hundreds of people at the hotel that night, I had to bump into an Australian! I remember going to my hotel room, having a conversation with God, and telling him, "Okay, okay, I get the message, enough already, now stop it!"

I finally made it to Australia, and now have a beautiful relationship with Rick, who is now my husband. Despite the fact that he has Huntington's disease, and his disease has progressed since I arrived, I know that my move here was "meant to be" so that I can be with Rick for the last part of his life.

—Mary Ferguson

WHAT ABOUT THOSE TIMES WHEN WE DON'T UNDERSTAND our meant-to-be moments? What if we struggle to interpret them, and can't discern whether we're meant to travel a new path or to stay the course? Whether the decision we're trying to make is major, as was Mary's move from America to Australia, or minor, we cannot underestimate the importance of not only asking for help, but for paying attention, and responding, even when we haven't asked for guidance.

According to an article by Tara Parker Pope in the March 10, 2010 issue of the New York Times, 82 percent of Americans "depend on God for help and guidance in making decisions." When Mary finally acknowledged and accepted God's guidance, she knew that choosing to be with Rick was the right decision. At times, it's a spiritual director or a trusted soul friend who provides that guidance, but sometimes, if we're paying close attention, it's a man in a T-shirt at a stoplight, offering clarity about how we might respond to our meant-to-be experiences.

CHAPTER 8

Ask for Comfort in Times of Anxiety and Grief

Sometimes, God's wisdom is present in our ordinary, everyday lives in ordinary, everyday ways. And sometimes Divine guidance comes to us subconsciously, even without direct petitioning. But where is God during the worst of times? How can we find the Divine in times of true anxiety and grief? Sometimes, just asking precedes our receiving what we most need.

A Thin Place Sign Brings Comfort

Marit and her sister, Kara, shared certain passages from *Thin Places*, my first book, with their mother during the month preceding her death. The three women were especially intrigued by the stories in which rainbows appeared soon after someone died, a phenomenon that grieving loved ones often find comforting. It's as if the deceased person somehow sends a sign that he or she is at peace, yet still with them in spirit. Marit and Kara hoped they, too, would receive a similar sign after their mother died, so they asked their mother for a thin place sign:

> I could talk forever about what kind of mom I had, what I believe she did for me and for those who knew her. But what assures me and restores me is what she last promised me.
>
> The afternoon before my mom died, as my sister and I lay in bed with her, I asked if she'd send us some sort of sign once she made it to heaven. "Will you come to us in our dreams, send us a rainbow or something? Some sign to let us know you made it?" She smiled and said she would. We had spoken for years about heaven and what it would be like, assuring ourselves that it would be glorious—a reward for the pain we lived through here on earth. We'd get to see the family we'd loved and lost, those whose loss has pained our hearts for so long. But once it was time to say goodbye to the most influential and important person in my life, doubts flooded me. I was paralyzed with the knowledge that I would never hold my mom again, never laugh with her, smell her, never feel the connection I have with her alone. My mom asked, "What if there is no heaven, honey? What if we are just dead, buried, and that's it?"
>
> "Maybe, Mom, but why not believe that there is something much better than this? Why not believe? Isn't that a better goodbye?" I held strong in spite of

my doubts. We all agreed and held one another in hope. Hope and memories were all we had.

After slipping into a coma for more than twelve hours, my mom died peacefully the next evening. Kara and I sat beside her the entire time. We held her, lay with her, sang to her, read stories, verses and poems to her. For a while we placed the phone next to her ear and let every one of her family members, including her own mother, whisper goodbye. We counted her breaths. We warmed her changing body. We hardly cried. It was surreal, unlike anything we could have ever anticipated. Slowly and deeply she took in her last breath and was no longer our mother. In front of us lay a body, an empty shell that had failed her for too many years. She was now within us. She was transformed and a part of who we had suddenly become. We were the oldest generation and the burden felt heavy, suddenly so much to do, and all of it on us. The burden lessened, though, by what happened just six days later.

The day of Mom's memorial service was a hot, sunny, dry day in Arizona. The drought had lasted more than three months. Almost a hundred and fifty people gathered in my sister's backyard after the church service, enjoying a feast and reliving stories about Mom.

My sister had arranged for balloons of every color to be launched by each person in hopes of "filling Mom's new room in heaven," a ritual she began when Kara had lost her darling daughter.

All at once, everyone let go of more than a hundred balloons. The sky filled with all the colors of the rainbow. It was an amazing sight. Just minutes later our cousin called out, "Look, there's a rainbow in the sky. Your mom is saying thank you!" We all ran to look and saw the most amazing rainbow circling the sun. Mom's rainbow was scientifically impossible, considering the lack of rain and its position around the sun. People wept, some fell to their knees. Doubters became believers. There wasn't a dry eye. Nothing could refute the grace of Mom's goodbye. Mom was already working the rainbow buttons and had, without a doubt, made it to heaven. And she chose the perfect time to tell us. She came to us, erasing our doubts. She was in heaven—and she deserved it more than anyone I've known. What she last promised was her greatest gift to me, and to my faith. Today, when I really need her, Mom continues to work her magic. I know she is always with me.

—MARIT

OTHERS WHO HAVE HEARD THE STORY OF MARIT'S GRANTED wish have said it comforts them; many even claim it has helped them be less fearful of death. Like Marit, we often experience meant-to-be moments during the most devastating times in our lives: before, during, and after the death of a loved one. Yet as was true for Marit, our prayers for comfort and peace are often answered in the midst of grief.

Joy in the Wake of Sorrow

Glenna faced the loss of her brother-in-law, Nick, while she and her daughter were both fighting life-threatening battles of their own. Several meant-to-be incidents occurred after Nick died. Finding a significant Scripture verse later helped Glenna acknowledge God's role in orchestrating the events that brought her and Nick's family comfort, peace, and joy:

> The end of 2008 and beginning of 2009 were especially difficult times for our family. My sister Dianne's husband, Nick, had been diagnosed with end-stage pancreatic cancer. The two of them were inseparable and had the kind of marriage that people dream about. He was still young, 65, and had always been the picture of health. Nick's death was a blow to all of us. He was a very holy, kind, and loving man. I couldn't keep from asking myself "Why now and why Nick?" During this same time my 31-year-old daughter, Sarah, was diagnosed with cervical cancer. This cancer can easily be cured in its early stages, but due to lack of insurance, she had not been going to the doctor for her checkups for quite some time. As a result, her cancer was advanced by the time it was found. She had a radical hysterectomy. Biopsies of the lymph nodes revealed the cancer had spread to both sides,

making this a Stage IIIB carcinoma. Within two weeks, she was undergoing chemotherapy once a week with daily radiation treatments to her pelvic area every Monday through Friday.

Nick was Sarah's godfather, and he was as desperately worried about her as she was about him. Once, when Sarah was having chemotherapy, she wanted to go see Nick in the hospital across the street, so I took her over to visit. They hugged each other and cried. They were both so sick and yet more concerned for each other than for themselves.

During Sarah's illness and Nick's illness, I found out I needed a hysterectomy and hernia repair. I held off until Sarah's treatment was done, and then had the surgery. My recovery was slow. So, although I did what I could, I was unable to help Sarah, or help my sister with Nick, as much as I wanted. The following March, Nick passed away peacefully, surrounded by his family.

Before all of this happened, I had registered to attend a healing touch/spiritual ministry and aromatherapy class. But when the time came, I felt I couldn't go because I was still so worn out from my surgery. However, even though I thought I should cancel, this still, small voice kept saying go, go, go—attend the class. So I went. Feeling miserable, I wondered if I would even make it to the end.

We were asked to pick out an essential oil for a healing touch technique called the Chakra connection to be practiced on us. The only oil that came up positive for me was a blend called "Joy." I was disappointed; I already had this oil at home and was hoping for something different, but I accepted it because I was too sick to argue. During the Chakra connection experience, I saw a bright light. Within this light, I saw a figure of a man with dark hair. I knew in my heart this man was Nick, who'd only been gone for eleven days. The same still, small voice in my mind that told me to come to class was now telling me that "Joy" was the gift Nick wanted to give me. It also told me how much I was loved. I felt Nick was saying that I give so much of myself to others that now it was time for me to take care of my own health. I began to cry. The feeling of love was so profound, beyond words, and the light grew brighter and brighter. I felt warmth and an incredible sense of peace and love. The pain in my body from the surgery disappeared, and in its place there was a profound sense of peace. I knew I had to tell my sister that Nick was okay, that he made it to heaven, and that he wanted her to have joy in her life as well.

Rushing to my car after class to tell my sister what had happened, I reached over to play a new CD by Alison Krauss I hadn't listened to yet. I turned it on and the CD skipped right to track four. I thought that was strange so took it out and put it back in, trying to get it to play the first song. Again it went to track four. I tried a third time with the same result. Finally I thought, "Oh well, I guess I'll just listen." I couldn't believe my ears. The song is called "Away Down the River." The lyrics conveyed a comforting message of hope. The song was so perfect and exactly what Nick would say to us if he could.

I brought my sister a sample of the "Joy" oil along with the song and told her my story. It turned out the number four, which was insignificant to me, was "their number." The next month in April (the fourth month) on Easter Sunday would have been their fortieth anniversary. Dianne said Nick always picked the number four for any identification numbers or passwords. We both began to cry. She said it was so like Nick to send this message to me. He loved and trusted me so much, knowing I would bring his message to her. It was truly an awesome experience as well as a comfort for my sister and me.

Later that night I opened the Bible randomly to Isaiah Chapter sixty-one. Verse three popped off the page. There it was, more proof: "To appoint unto them that mourn in Zion, to give unto them beauty for ashes, the oil of joy for mourning, the garment of praise for the spirit of heaviness; that they might be called trees of righteousness, the planting of the Lord, that he might be glorified" (Isaiah 61:3, New American Standard). I immediately called my sister and we laughed and cried, both believing with all our hearts that this experience came from above.

— GLENNA BELLAND

Unexpected Gifts

M.G.'s prayers throughout the days leading up to her mother's death were, she admits, "half-hearted requests for heavenly gifts." But she certainly didn't expect them to be taken seriously. Her experiences also demonstrate that it's okay to ask for signs from our deceased loved ones. How could these requests be granted without the existence of a loving God who enables them to occur? Each time they happen, it's an affirmation of God's promise in scripture that love never dies. Her story:

> My mother was diagnosed with non-Hodgkin's lymphoma in 1991. She went through chemotherapy, which was successful enough to give her two years of remission before it returned, this time in her bones. Then she got pneumonia and spent the last two months of her life in the hospital, where we all experienced a roller coaster of emotions and events. So many "thin place" moments took place during that time. Then after she died, we continued to experience more gifts from her in our lives. We even saw rainbows when there was no rain!
>
> Here are just some of the things that happened: On July Fourth that year, Mom took a turn for the worse. The medical staff told my dad and me she probably would not make it through the night. We called the rest of the family to come to the hospital to say good-bye. The priest was called to come give her a final blessing. The hospital priest we

knew could not come, but another priest came in his place. He said his name was Father Peregrine; we had never heard of him. But Dad and I were shocked when we heard his name. My dad and mom had prayed to St. Peregrine, the patron saint for cancer.

My mom did make it through that night but remained on a respirator for a long time. When she was able to speak, she told us about Ed and Ann, her aunt and uncle who had been dead for many years. There was no doubt in our minds she had seen them the night she was so close to death.

As we were saying our goodbyes to her three days before she died, I asked whose bald head would I rub when she was gone (I used to stand by her bed and rub her fuzzy bald head). I jokingly said maybe she could send me a bald-headed man. I was 43, single, and never married. She joked back, "Or maybe one with lots of hair." I have now been married for nine years to a man with a very thick head of hair. I met him shortly after she died. Thank you, Mom!

I had a very hard time with Mom's death, since I didn't have a family to focus on like my other siblings had. I believe that's why Mom came to me in a dream one night. Even though I don't remember the details, her presence was so real it continues to be a comfort to me. Then the morning after the dream on my way to work, an eagle flew right over my car, not ten feet from it. I have never seen an eagle that close or in that area. That eagle all but said, "Hi from Mom!"

At the time of Mom's death, my sister had been trying to get pregnant for a couple years. She had been on some fertility pills, but stopped them while Mom was ill. Just two months after my mother died, she became pregnant with her first child. She asked for a baby, and now she has four children—without any additional drugs to help her get pregnant.

With my marriage, my sister's babies, and all the "thin place" moments, we often talk about Mom sending us so many blessings. My oldest sister now says, "I didn't know we were asking for things! I thought we were just saying goodbye!"

—M.G.

A Prayer for Kenny

Sometimes we are prompted to ask God to help someone without knowing why. Through intercessory prayer, we pray on behalf of others, such as Kathy did for her twin brother, Kenny, when he was thousands of miles away.

Kathy and her husband, Tim, awoke at the same time in the middle of the night and both "were impressed by the Holy Spirit to pray for Kenny. We both knew it simultaneously. This was odd as we were busy parents of small children with full days, and Kenny at that time wasn't in our daily lives of thought or conversation." But they responded. "Pray, pray, pray we did, not knowing why."

Within a day or two, Kathy's mother received word that Kenny's helicopter had crashed, at about the same time they were praying. Her brother was well-trained in air-water survival and took all the right steps to save the crew and himself. Fortunately all four crewmembers got out and were rescued before the helicopter went down.

Kathy isn't sure their rescue was miraculous because her brother and his crew were very prepared to respond to an accident like this one. Yet, as she says, "As close and connected as I feel to my twin brother, the marvel for me was of the wonderful working power of the Holy Spirit to impress us, get through to us, move us to pray when my twin on the other side of the world was in crisis and prayer was needed."

Prayers of Protection

Gary, a charismatic Christian, had a feeling that a good friend of his, Sam, was in trouble. He wasn't sure what had happened, but he "just knew" something was wrong. So he began praying to the Holy Spirit, in tongues, for Sam. After some time in prayer, Gary eventually felt at peace and knew he could relax.

The following day he learned his friend had been in a car accident. The crash destroyed the car, but his friend walked away without a scratch. Gary believes his prayers protected his friend from harm.

CHAPTER 9

Acknowledge Divine Providence with Gratitude

REFLECTING UPON THE MEANING AND THE IMPACT OF "meant-to-be" moments often results in offering gratitude to the God who is so actively involved in our lives. As this chapter shows, the practice of gratitude acknowledges God's presence and guidance. Gratitude is one of the most important aspects of living a full and happy life.

Within days after my father died of lung cancer, a friend sent me a sympathy card containing these words by German theologian Dietrich Bonhoeffer from his book, *Letters and Papers from Prison:*

> Nothing can make up for the absence of someone we love. . . . It is nonsense to say that God fills the gap; God doesn't fill it, but on the contrary, God keeps it empty, and so helps us keep alive our former communion with each other, even at the cost of pain. . . . The dearer and richer our memories, the more difficult the separation. But gratitude

changes the pangs of memory into a tranquil joy. The beauties of the past are borne, not as a thorn in the flesh, but as precious gifts in themselves.

Our family found Bonhoeffer's words so hopeful and so meaningful that we included them in Dad's funeral program. And we did find "tranquil joy" as we recalled countless fond memories of our father, and all too soon, those of our mother. But in the years since their deaths, we've also felt grateful for the thin-place experiences and meant-to-be moments that comforted us, affirmed our faith, and fostered hope.

Gratitude enabled us to acknowledge God's presence in the midst of our grief.

Home Safe

Gratitude also enabled Dave Norby to be comforted by God when he experienced not just one, but three meant-to-be moments after the sudden loss of his son. He felt reassured after each experience that his son was not just safe but happy in his heavenly home.

The doorbell rang at 12:30 a.m. on April 22, 2008. The young woman at the door asked if we were the parents of Benjamin David Norby. Then she said the words no parent wants to hear: "I am so sorry to tell you that Ben died this evening in Huntington Beach."

The next morning, on Wednesday, April 23, I woke up at 6:30 in the morning. I felt I should get up and walk downstairs. As I walked down the steps, I felt a tug to go into the guest room. There is a bookshelf to the left as you enter the room; on the top shelf is a big white Bible my mom had given me ten years earlier. I had never read it and had completely forgotten the Bible was even there.

I walked to the bookshelf, pulled the Bible down, and laid it on the old chest in front of the couch. I opened the front cover of the Bible and found a program from my older brother's 1968 confirmation day; the program was forty years old.

I read the program and saw that the verse my brother had memorized for his confirmation was John 3:16. I opened the Bible and began to read the verse: "For God so loved the world that he gave his one and only Son, that whoever believes in him shall not perish but have eternal life." (John 3:16 NIV). As I began reading, a deep sense of peace flowed over me. With every word I read, my sense of peace grew even stronger, and I had this overwhelming feeling that my son, Ben, was in heaven and happier than I could begin to understand.

When I finished reading John 3:16, the pillow leaning against the back of the couch to my left tipped over and made a loud thud. The thud was as if someone had slapped the pillow with his or her hand. At that moment, an intense sensation that

Ben was in heaven with Jesus flowed through my mind and body. It was amazing to say the least. I felt grateful for such a crystal-clear message, affirming my belief that Ben was safe and at peace.

The following afternoon, I was walking our dog Taquito in Shapell Park. It was a beautiful clear and sunny day. As I often do, I took the leash off Taquito because she never leaves my side. As we entered Shapell Park, Taquito took off running as fast as she could toward the opposite side of the park.

I was grieving deeply and was in no mood for chasing after the dog. However, I had no choice but to run after her. As I ran I noticed that on the opposite end of the park, about a hundred and fifty yards away, was an adult with a small child and a baby in a stroller. Taquito has poor eyesight and cannot even see a rabbit fifty feet away, so for her to race across the park towards them was amazing.

When I arrived, I noticed the young man had deep blue eyes and looked flawless. His hair, skin, clothes, and shoes—everything about him was perfect. I apologized to him because Taquito chased his son around the stroller until I picked the dog up. The man was extremely kind and calm, without any concern that Taquito was chasing his child.

Once I had Taquito in my arms, I felt prompted to ask the man if the baby in the stroller was a boy or girl. He told me the baby was a girl. Then I felt a strong urge to ask him what her name was, so I did. The man told me his child's name was Faith! The instant that he told me her name was Faith, a sensation of peace flowed into my mind and body just like the day before, and I knew Ben was safe.

Then, on March 27, 2009, almost a year after Ben passed on, I had a dream early in the morning, a dream so intense it woke me up. In my dream, Ben came to me and gave me a hug, his face filled with amazing peace, happiness, and joy. I wrapped my arms around my son and hugged him hard. I felt his back muscles and rib bones on my fingertips and hands.

Ben was perfect, Ben was happy, Ben was free, and Ben was filled with joy. I woke up, said a prayer, and thanked God for the dream and gift of hugging Ben. Then I fell back asleep.

When I reawakened at 6:30 to the alarm, I shared the dream with my wife, Joni. She was happy and touched that I had a visit from Ben in my dream. Then she said she wished she could have such an experience or a sign.

Joni and I rarely sit together at the table for breakfast, but that morning I felt I wanted to do just that. While we were eating, I again shared my dream with her and told her that Ben was very happy and safe. Joni smiled gratefully and said gently, but with sadness, that she wished she could get a sign Ben was safe.

At that very moment, the chandelier above the kitchen table started to swing back and forth very slowly. I looked at the digital clock on the oven to my left; it was 7:31 a.m. I stood up and checked the other hanging chandelier in the dining room; it was still, as was the one in the entryway. *It isn't an earthquake*, I thought to myself.

I sat back down and we continued to eat our cereal with the chandelier continuing to swing back and forth. We would look down at the cereal; eat a little, then look up at the light until our cereal was gone. Finally Joni reached up and stopped the chandelier from swinging. "I want Ben back, not a swinging chandelier," she said. Yet, I felt peace flow through my mind and body again, knowing our son is with God in heaven.

God's grace has been an amazing gift during my grief. The pain of losing our son Ben is beyond words. The sorrow is hard to bear and the grief is very draining; it's a very slow process each day. And yet when I ask God to comfort me, God gives me peace. Little by little, I am beginning to heal. I miss my son very much, but I am certain that his spirit is alive and well.

I am very grateful that I have these experiences to share, reflect on, and remind me that Benny is at peace in heaven and that I will be with him again when I pass on. I know God is within every living being. He is with you and me right now. God is everywhere that love exists.

—Dave Norby

IT TOOK TONI SEVERAL YEARS TO UNDERSTAND AND BE grateful for the gift her beloved uncle gave her upon his death:

> I grew up in a typical small town. My father was the youngest of ten children. Most of his siblings lived within walking distance of our home. My parents couldn't afford their own home so we stayed with my grandfather, my Dad's father, in a corner row house, until his death when I was ten.
>
> Dad's sister, my Aunt Mary, and her husband, my Uncle Sam, lived right next door. Mary and Sam were unable to have children of their own, but since my brothers and I lived next door, they were like our second parents. I was particularly close to Sam. At the time, I'd probably say I was closer to Sam than to my own father.
>
> Unfortunately, when I was twelve, Sam died of a pulmonary embolism. On the night he passed, he came to me. Asleep in my bed, he woke me to say good-bye. I didn't see him but I did most assuredly hear him, and I knew that he had died and was leaving us. I started crying and begging him not to go. I absolutely know that it was hard for him as well. A few minutes later the phone rang, I could hear my mother get out of bed, descend the stairs, pick up the phone, and say, "Oh God, no." With that I knew I'd lost Uncle Sam.

People say that something good can be found even in bad things. But I couldn't find the good in Sam's death. That night my life changed forever. I never stopped feeling sorry for myself that I lost him. Then one night while I was in nursing school "the good" came to me. The gift Sam had given me was coming to me before he passed over. Sam gave me the assurance that there is life after death—a gift beyond measure. My life has truly never been the same since I realized what I'd been given. Sam's gift has stayed with me through thirty-six years of nursing practice. It has made all the difference.

I share Sam's story with all my terminal patients, and I ask that they give him my love when they meet him in heaven.

My Uncle Sam resides where hope dwells, and loves me still.

—TONI BRUSH

SOME MEANT-TO-BE INCIDENTS ELICIT OUR GRATITUDE TO those who are like human angels, acting as channels of love and compassion when we most need it. An example of this devotion is the caring nurse's aide who was present at the bedside of Nora's dying elderly mother. Nora wrote the following letter to the director of the nursing home in gratitude for the loving care given to her mother, especially at the time of her death:

My mother, Shirley Goldlust, passed away this morning on Fairmount Two. I'm sure I'm not the first, nor will I be the last, to bestow accolades on the entire Menorah Park organization. From the very start, almost three years ago, I've received nothing but compassion and individual consideration for my mother's needs. Menorah Park is a superb facility, with attention to immaculate living conditions and a unique staff that exemplifies what an extended family should be. My gratitude and appreciation can never be fully expressed in words. I can only say that after my visits with Mother, as I left with the ever-present music from the player piano in the lobby accompanying me, I always had the comforting sense that she was truly in the sturdy hands of angels.

Everyone, from the housekeeping staff, the social activities people, the aides and nurses, religious staff, social workers, hospice staff, up to Dr. Knight and Dr. Polish, the administrators, always had a nice word and a soft touch to share with my mother.

The purpose of this letter is to reveal a very special moment I had this morning as I was alone with my mother in her room a few minutes after she passed. Sadly, I had not been there at the exact moment, but arrived shortly after. An aide was watching over her, waiting for me to arrive. The room was softly lit with a dim lamp; my mother's body was calm, at peace, and lying in a pristine bed. The aide softly gave me her condolences and left.

I began to brush my mother's hair and wash her face when I noticed a red smudge mark on her cheekbone. As I swept over it with the damp washcloth, I realized it was lipstick from a kiss. This simple whisper of an act told me that while she was leaving this world there was someone at her side who, in their own private moment, cared enough about my mother to send her off with a final act of love. No one was watching; there was no relative or supervisor to impress. It was an act borne of pure, innate compassion. This kindness can't be taught or learned through schooling. It's there from the heart. And the magic of Menorah Park is its ability to find people who care enough about the residents to accompany them on their final journey.

I was en route when I was told my mom had passed, driving frantically and cursing myself for not being there sooner. I ran into her room full of remorse and sorrow that I wasn't there when she took her final breath. But all those feelings dissolved when I realized someone was there who cared enough to kiss her good-bye.

Please tell your staff that these small acts of compassion don't go unnoticed. I will forever remember the love and dignity shown to Mother during her stay at Menorah Park.

—NORA GIGLIO

GRATITUDE IS ONE OF THE MOST IMPORTANT ASPECTS OF living a full and happy life. Reflecting on our experiences often results in gratitude to the Higher Power who responds to what we have asked for, and is so actively involved in our lives. A daily practice of gratitude helps reveal God's presence and guidance. That revelation results in the ultimate soul friendship with God, which can lead to a deeper and more rewarding existence as we learn to live each day as if it were our last—and our best.

STEP IV

Say Yes!: Responding to Meant-to-be Moments

FOLLOWING STEP FOUR ENCOURAGES US TO SAY "YES" TO opportunities we receive to live life fully by being a channel of love to others and loving ourselves more deeply. We thus become the person we are meant to be, by fulfilling God's most important commandment: to "love the Lord your God with all your heart, and with all your soul, and with all your strength, and with all your mind. And love your neighbor as yourself." (Luke 10:27, NIV)

In the Scripture verse "Be still and know I am God," (Psalm 46:10, NIV) we are invited to *be* still so we can hear and reflect upon God's messages to us. We also can find God in the meant-to-be moments that enable us to *be* comforted, inspired, filled with hope, and affirmed in faith. Other times, God calls us to "do" something. Thus some of the most significant moments occur when we respond with a "Yes" to something we are prompted to do. By saying "Yes," we deepen our relationship with ourselves, with others and with God. In so doing, we discover our purpose, our reason for being.

CHAPTER 10

Say "Yes" By Extending Love to Ourselves and Others

Finding A Soul Mate

For Sue, asking for what she wanted, then paying attention and heeding her intuition, enabled her to say "Yes" to the opportunity to give and receive love from the man who became her soul mate:

> No one plans to get a divorce. When you say those vows on your wedding day, you expect to live happily ever after. Unfortunately, when I said my vows I didn't figure substance and physical abuse would be part of the equation. Still, it took several years for me to have the courage to end the cycle of abuse and leave my marriage.
>
> Suddenly I found myself a single mother of a 3-year-old son and 1-year-old daughter. We were the three amigos; my children were there for me just as much as I was there for them. Each night after I tucked them in, I would pray, "God please send

me my soul mate. It's obvious that I did a lousy job finding him on my own. I promise to pay attention and be present. Amen." I prayed this prayer for two years, the entire time dating on and off. No sparks occurred. I often asked myself if I was paying enough attention.

Then on a Thursday evening in 1994, tired after a long day at work, I caved to the kids' plea to eat at the Golden Arches. My girlfriend and I brought our kids for dinner and the promise of Playland. We settled in and as I scanned the room, there he was. I locked eyes with my soul mate. At that moment, I got an overwhelming feeling I was going to marry this complete stranger. I even told my girlfriend. Of course, she thought I was nuts. For the next hour, he and I kept glancing at each other. I knew with certainty that my life was going to change.

As he began to pack his boys up to head home, I panicked. I realized I might never see him again! My girlfriend prodded me to go introduce myself and find out if he was even available. So I wrote my work number on a napkin, folded it, and headed in his direction. He was seated in the French Fry chair, and as I slid into the Grimace chair, the conversation went like this:

Me: "Hi. I'm going out on a limb here, but are you married?"

Him: "Hi. No, I am divorced."

Me: "Phew! Me too. Would you like to go out sometime?"

Him: "Sure, I'd like that."

We chatted a bit and as I stood to go I slid him the napkin with my work number. He called the next day and we went on our first date the following weekend. We married eight months later and we recently celebrated our seventeenth wedding anniversary.

I thank God every day for answering my prayer; I am so grateful I paid attention and said "Yes" to the opportunity to introduce myself to the love of my life.

—SUE

One Grieving Daughter Comforts Another

While waiting for a lung transplant, the mother of one of Marit's friends died. It happened just a few days before the elderly woman was scheduled to move into a smaller home. As a favor to her friend, Marit offered to pack up the woman's possessions while the family attended their mother's funeral.

Despite her good intentions, Marit found the task difficult. She was filled with sadness as she remembered how hard it had been to go through her own mother's belongings just four short months earlier. By saying "yes" to this task and to the opportunity to reach out to another grieving daughter, her actions brought comfort and peace to both of them:

It was an emotional time for me, packing up her things and deciding what gets thrown, what gets set aside for the kids, what gets kept for further discussion. I looked at prescription bottles, pads, soaps, and candies—things bought for future use. I looked through her Day-Timer, her unchecked Lotto tickets, her "to do" list, her appointments scheduled for the coming week. It was a lot to take in, to say the least. Then, I was done and I left.

I felt very somber, reliving what I had just done for my own mom, four months ago to the day. So, as any reasonable girl would do, I went to a salon for a manicure and pedicure to cheer myself up. Believe it or not, it was at the salon where I found a thin-place moment.

I went to the first nail salon I saw, one I had never been to before. It was a dump; dirty and cluttered. But I went anyway because I was tired, stressed, and in need of comforting. I wanted to sit in a recliner chair and have someone rub my feet. My cell phone rang. It was one of my dearest and oldest friends. She had lost her mom two years ago and I began to tell her about my day—how I'd relived all of the painful moments of parting with my mom's things. I spoke about the emotional impact of seemingly meaningless things. She told me I was insane to have offered to help pack up a strange woman's things so close to my mother's death. What was I thinking, subjecting myself to such suffering?

Sitting next to me was another client, the only other one there. A pretty young woman, she was well-dressed and groomed, nice but not particularly friendly in her gestures or glances toward me. When I hung up the phone, she apologized and told me that she was sorry but she couldn't help overhearing the conversation. She asked if I had lost my mom recently. I told her, "Yes, about four months ago."

She then told me she had lost her mom on Wednesday.

"Wednesday—you mean two days ago?" I asked.

As she nodded, tears glistened in her eyes. We sat there, oblivious to the nail techs, the noise, the fans, and the radio. We talked and cried. We shared our stories and our faith. I told her about my mom's rainbow, her sign from heaven that she'd made it there. I told her to believe she'll see her own mom again, to look up, to seek the signs, the "thin place moments." I probably had no right to place my beliefs on her, but it just felt right, very real and "meant to be." It felt completely reasonable to tell her that her mom sees her and made it to heaven, too.

As I got up to leave, I noticed tears running down her face. I was numb. I didn't even know her name, but I hugged her like she was my sister. I sensed her pain and also her longing to feel peace, even if only for a moment. I told her to keep getting pedicures and keep putting makeup on because those few minutes of looking pretty might just be the best moments she'll have for a while. I told her to keep hoping, keep looking, for signs to appear.

When I got into my car, it seemed as if I was abandoning her. I felt like I needed to do more to help her along this path, though I had no idea where it would lead. So I wrote down my name and number and ran back in. To make light of the awkward moment, I told her I felt like I was asking her out on a date, and told her to call me when things settled down and we could go for a cup of coffee. She was still crying but she seemed thankful for my return and my phone number.

I felt proud when she told me that God had put me in her life, right at that moment, exactly when she needed me. Maybe, just maybe, I was a thin place for her that day. It was as if her mom used me to tell her daughter to look for the signs that would let her know her mother had "made it" and was now at peace.

—MARIT

WHEN PEOPLE ARE MINDFUL OF WHAT IS HAPPENING IN their own lives—especially incidents that seem meant to be—they make them meaningful by the way in which they respond to them. Not every experience invites a response. But many, like Marit's, do. By choosing to respond, she helped both the other woman and herself find hope and comfort in the midst of their grief. Marit's response enabled her to find meaning and the comfort of God's presence when she needed it most. By choosing to reach out compassionately to a stranger, her personal pain was transformed into an act of love. And that love helped both women heal.

The Marble Lady

We never know when the chance to show love to another person will present itself, but when we open our hearts to the possibilities, the opportunities are there, especially after we ask for them. That was true for Cathy, "the Marble Lady," who helped a distressed mother find the perfect last-minute Christmas gift for her daughter:

> I was a stay-at-home mother of five facing an upcoming divorce. Without a completed college degree, I scraped by financially by waitressing, housecleaning, and doing childcare. However, I was still trying to set an example of community service for my children, so I was doing presentations about marble play at schools free of charge. I also was researching and working on a simple little booklet to help preserve the wholesome, traditional game of marbles. Having put aside my quarters from my waitressing tips for over a year, I finally was able to self-publish my small booklet, *Knuckles Down: A Fun Guide to Marble Play*. I could afford to print only one thousand copies, but I planned to donate

many of them to grade-school libraries and histori-
cal societies because at the time, you couldn't find
marbles at stores anymore, and there was very little
information available in research materials about
them. Quite literally, Americans were about to lose
their marbles!

One day, just as I was backing out of the drive-
way to go to work, the UPS truck turned in and
delivered my first box of the marble books. I was
in a rush, so I threw them in the trunk of my car
and went on to the restaurant. That night I had a
table of twelve people from all over the United
States. They were a lively group! I asked them what
brought them all together and they said I wouldn't
believe them if they told me. "I've got five children,"
I said. "Try me!" They said they were there for a
marbles auction! When I told them I had just written a book on marbles, I saw two of the men wink at
each other as if they didn't believe me and thought
I was just going for a bigger tip. I took their orders,
then ran out the back door to my car and grabbed a
book from the box in the trunk. I served them their
drinks along with a copy of my book. The women in
the group cheered and the members of the Marble
Collectors Society of America bought two hundred
and fifty of my books that night! They also invited
me to speak at their upcoming Boston convention.

It was meant to be. My books arrived just as I
was heading to work, where I waitressed just one
night a week. My serving section was swamped,

but the boss asked me to take on the big group from another section, saying that if anyone could handle them, I could. They weren't staying at our hotel and had come to our restaurant because they were tired of the food at their hotel down the street. And that night was only the beginning. Several marble miracles have occurred that continue to answer my prayers many times over.

One of those miracles happened while I was alone organizing marbles in my marble room. I plainly heard a voice direct me to put together a beautiful bag of marbles. I looked up to see who spoke to me but no one was there. Nevertheless, the voice had been so clear that I got my finest drawstring velvet bag with embroidered flowers on it and filled it with beautiful marbles. I carried that bag around for the next three or four days, not knowing why. Then, just three days before Christmas, a meeting at church was cancelled due to a child's illness. Since I had some extra time before my next meeting, I went across the street to the Dollar Store to look for last-minute Christmas items.

While I was in line waiting to pay for my things, a woman came rushing into the store and asked the clerk where their marbles were. He apologetically told her they had no marbles. She insisted they must have some marbles and again he apologized and told her they had none. At that point, she started to cry. I tapped her on the shoulder and said, "Ma'am, I have some marbles you can have."

Between her sobs she asked who I was. As I took the bag from my purse I told her, "I'm the Marble Lady!" Seeing the marbles, she sobbed even harder and asked for my email so she could explain later because she had to rush off right then.

That night I received an email from her:

Dearest Marble Lady,

My little girl, Michaela, is our adopted daughter. We just finalized her adoption on the fourth of November. While in foster care, she experienced horrendous physical, sexual, and mental abuse no one should ever experience, let alone a three-year-old child. Michaela came to live with us at age three and a half, and is now five years old. She has made tremendous progress and continues to progress and heal daily. She is pure, non-materialistic, and she loves the Lord.

For the last week, I have been looking all over town for marbles for her. That's all she wants for Christmas— just marbles! I looked everywhere, but I couldn't find them anywhere. I was very upset. The night before I saw you, I prayed that the dear Lord would help me find marbles for my little girl. The next day, something told me to go to the Dollar Store, and you know the rest of the story. Now, how many times have you been in line at the Dollar Store needing marbles, and the lady behind you happens to have a bag of them in her purse? This was Divine intervention and you were an angel for my daughter this Christmas. I can't thank you enough!"

I keep her email in my journal, and ever since I received it, I ask God in my daily morning prayer to help me tune in to anyone nearby that might need my help! That prayer has been answered over and over; I have learned not to question that still, small voice when it speaks to me! And, I've stayed connected with Michaela's mom, who says that she still plays with her marbles. I will be sending Michaela a very special bag this Christmas!

—Cathy Svacina

Coincidental Connections

Sometimes, our encounters with others aren't particularly dramatic, yet are still very meaningful. That was the case for Laurie, who believes that her connections with others are meant to be.

One afternoon many years ago, Laurie (my co-worker) and I were discussing how synchronicity and intuition seemed to help us live more fully. When I asked about her own experiences, she said, "Actually, I just had one last night."

Laurie had been on an airplane, returning from a business trip. Only one other person was seated in first class, but for some reason they had been placed next to each other. Laurie was about to get up and move to another seat when she sneezed. The man said "God bless you" in such a pleasant way that she decided to stay put and visit with him.

They discovered they both worked in the advertising business and had many common acquaintances. The man was searching for a new job. True to her thoughtful disposition, Laurie brainstormed with him about possible job opportunities in their common field. By the time the plane landed, she had made a new friend and had promised to assist him in his job search. By the following afternoon, as she was speaking to me, Laurie already had made several calls to her network of industry friends on behalf of her new friend and had passed on a couple of promising leads to him. She felt certain they met so she could help him find a job.

On another occasion, she was contacted by an employment recruiter who wondered if she might be interested in a new position. Although she was not interested herself, after hanging up the phone, she remembered a former client, a woman she didn't know very well, but someone she enjoyed. Laurie hadn't talked to the woman in many months, but Laurie intuitively felt she might be looking for a new job.

Laurie reached across her desk for her Rolodex file, intending to look up the woman's phone number to call her. Just then, her computer beeped. A message had arrived from the woman she was about to contact, just to say hi. Laurie told the woman about the recruiter's phone call, and the woman was excited enough to ask for the recruiter's phone number.

Over the many years of our friendship, Laurie has described numerous other examples of little opportunities she has been given to help others. Many times, she has experienced a telepathic prompting to call others without knowing the specific reason for her call. Other times, she feels someone needs her help but is not sure who, so she will flip through her Rolodex file until a name pops out at her. She responds to these promptings and is amazed how often these people say they were "just thinking about her," or needed a sympathetic ear.

When asked if she believed it was possible she was being directed by some higher power when these coincidences occur, Laurie, who grew up in the Protestant faith, responded that she now considers herself an agnostic. She is uncertain about her beliefs, but she does not deny the possibility that God exists. However, she recognizes that these "chance meetings and experiences," her willingness to respond to them, as well as the assistance she provides to others, have added a dimension to her life that would otherwise be absent. When she moved to Minneapolis several ago, she started a nonprofit social group that helps relocated professionals build friendships. The group has been the catalyst for at least eighteen marriages, including her own, as well as innumerable friendships.

Laurie exemplifies how, when one is alert for ways to be of service to others, we can have a positive impact on others and live fully ourselves. She says the awareness that a higher power might be using her to help others has "transformed her life," giving her a sense of purpose. She has learned that the more she notices and responds to these opportunities, the more of them she is given.

Promises to Keep

For Kathy's mother, who was recovering from surgery to remove a brain tumor, the choice she faced was literally life or death:

> The rain had passed through town earlier in the day. Gray clouds still blocked the sun, although at times a ray or two of bright light would reach down from the sky.
>
> "Hon, I'm going out for groceries." My father spoke softly as his hand reached for the front screen door and pushed it open.
>
> My mother was resting on the couch. "Don't be too long."
>
> "It will only take an hour. You rest." Father shook his head, worry casting shadows over his face. The doctors said the operation was successful, but the recovery had been slow. Sixteen hours of delicate surgery to remove a tumor wrapped around the inside of her head, and then days of unconsciousness. Mom was home, but needed rest to rebuild her strength. He wondered, would she be strong enough to complete the recovery process or would she give up and leave him?
>
> Mom brought her legs up onto the couch and laid her head down on a pillow. It would be pleasant to rest on the couch and wait for her beloved to return. Soon afterward her papa joined her. He stood in front of her, motioning for her to come to

him. It was her papa as she had last seen him over thirty years ago, at the time of his death. He had died young. She had already lived on earth longer than he had. He'd been gone so long, yet there he was, standing in front of her and asking her to join him.

He never spoke to her, but she knew what he wanted. He stretched out his hand toward her and she raised her hand toward him. Their fingers were just about to touch when she heard the handle of the front door turn and my dad call out, "Hon', I'm home."

She knew she had a choice to make—take hold of papa's hand or return to her husband.

Dropping her outstretched arm, Mother sat up and smiled as her husband brought the grocery bags into the house.

She always will know that her papa's gentle presence waits for her on the other side. He is waiting and biding his time until he can reach out his hand and bring her to join him. He won't force her to come, but when the time is right, he will be there to assist her in the transition. Until then, she has said "Yes" to life.

—Kathy Johnson

Divine Guidance and a
Life-Saving Reunion

After reconnecting with Jeanne, her former therapist, Carrie also said "Yes" to life, despite an earlier temptation to say "No." As Carrie's counselor during the mid-1980s, Jeanne had helped her cope with some of the most significant times in Carrie's life: marriage, the birth of three children, and then many years later, a heartbreaking divorce and devastating custody battle. After helping Carrie navigate these difficult crises, Jeanne did not see her for more than twenty years. Recently, they reunited after three meant-to-be experiences "nudged" Carrie to reconnect with the woman who would help save her life.

After her last formal therapy session with Jeanne, Carrie continued to struggle with getting through each day. She lost her job, her family and her home. Filled with despair, she also had lost hope. Believing the future would not get any better, thoughts of suicide plagued her. She had long since ceased to see Jeanne professionally, yet three times within a few months, Carrie "just happened to see Jeanne from a distance" although Jeanne didn't see her. The first time, she saw Jeanne having lunch with someone at a restaurant. Then just weeks later, Carrie caught a glimpse of her through a hole in a fence near Jeanne's home. When Carrie spotted Jeanne the third time, at a store in the Mall of America, she wondered if God was trying to let her know that Jeanne could help her. Remembering that Jeanne had provided invaluable guidance and support all those years ago, Carrie decided to visit her former therapist once again.

Moments before Carrie knocked on the door of her home office, Jeanne had finished her final therapy session for the day. She was headed out to another appointment, with her jacket on, keys in one hand and the other hand about to turn the knob of her front door. After hearing a knock, she opened the door and saw a sobbing woman facing her. At first, she didn't recognize Carrie; it had been over twenty years since they had last visited in person. But when she spoke and said her name, Jeanne immediately recognized Carrie's voice. She invited her inside. Had Carrie knocked a few minutes earlier, Jeanne wouldn't have answered the door because she was seeing a client. Five minutes later, and Jeanne would not have been home. Both Carrie and Jeanne now believe their reunion was "meant to be."

Carrie explained how she was "at the end of her rope" and was contemplating suicide. Seeing Jeanne three times seemed like Divine Guidance reminding Carrie of the invaluable counseling Jeanne previously provided to her. With this insight, Carrie realized Jeanne might be the one person who could help her again. As they were speaking, Jeanne's daughter Amy came home. Amy had known Carrie personally years earlier, so she also offered to help Carrie as a caring friend as well.

Before leaving Jeanne's home, Carrie committed to seeing her therapist again on a regular basis until she became healthy and strong. At fifty years old, she now regards her challenges and struggles as "turning points" instead of reasons to end her life. With the help of a capable and kind therapist, and the God who guided her back to Jeanne, Carrie has said "Yes" to doing whatever she can to live as fully as possible.

A Sister's Loving Gift

Lynn and Cheryl are soul friends as well as sisters. Their relationship became even stronger after Lynn helped give Cheryl and her husband Hank the most precious gift imaginable: a child. Motivated by love, and several incidents that seemed "meant to be," Lynn's decision to say "yes" finally enabled Cheryl and Hank to fulfill their dream of becoming parents.

For nearly fourteen years, Lynn watched Cheryl's heart break each time one of her six sisters became pregnant then had a healthy baby. None of them had any problem conceiving except for Cheryl, the seventh of nine siblings. The one time Cheryl had become pregnant, she suffered a miscarriage. After Cheryl eventually learned she was unable to carry a child to full term, one of her sisters generously offered to be a gestational carrier. But that effort also failed.

By the time Cheryl and Hank reached their mid-forties, they finally accepted the apparent reality that they would never have their own biological children. The couple asked their parents and siblings to respect their decision. It was just too painful after the procedure failed the first time.

Despite Cheryl's insistence that she and Hank were "Okay with their situation," Lynn believed something still could be done for them. Her determination to help the couple was fueled by several things that simply "fell into place."

First, when Lynn and Cheryl's fifty-two-year-old sister, Judy, and her husband decided to have another child, they first checked with Judy's physician to see if she was physically able to safely get pregnant. Various tests affirmed she was still fertile and healthy enough to carry a child. Judy delivered twins a year later. This happy event caused Lynn, who was nearly ten years younger than Judy, to believe she might be able to carry Cheryl's child.

Second, Lynn was about to complete a two-year contracted position. In a few months, she would be laid off. Therefore, she could take some time to go through the necessary fertility procedures and, hopefully, become pregnant before starting another job.

Third, Lynn's insurance deductible had already been satisfied for the rest of the year. This meant that the cost of fertility testing, pregnancy and delivery would all be covered by her insurance.

After recognizing these favorable circumstances, Lynn visited both a perinatal doctor and her regular physician to be screened as a potential surrogate mother. She did this without telling Cheryl. After being assured she was physically able to carry a child, Lynn told Cheryl and Hank that she wanted to try to become pregnant, using the two embryos left from the couple's previous efforts to become parents. At first, Cheryl and Hank said "No" to Lynn's loving offer. The pain and disappointment they had already endured made them fearful of being hurt again.

They also expressed concern about Lynn's own family.

Because Lynn was a single mother with two children, ages seven and nine, they worried about the physical, emotional and financial repercussions a pregnancy would have on their lives. Despite Lynn's insistence that it would work out, the couple resisted her offer for the next two months.

Meanwhile, Lynn's mother and other sisters also wanted to do whatever they could to help Cheryl and Hank have a child. After learning about Lynn's offer, they told her they would support her family with whatever they needed, financially and emotionally. Then the women told Cheryl about their promise to Lynn. Despite their concern for Lynn's family, and for their own emotional well-being if this effort failed, Cheryl and Hank finally agreed to accept Lynn's offer.

For the next several months, many remarkable people appeared in Lynn's life for various reasons. As she now says, "everyone who touched my life, physically or figuratively, was amazing." One of the most special people was Dr. B., a fertility specialist. After extensive testing and legal and psychiatric counseling, Lynn was deemed a suitable candidate surrogacy by Dr. B. who promised, "Once I recommend you, I don't fail."

The process of getting pregnant was not easy. Lynn had to administer several shots to herself daily, putting her body into a premenopausal state so it wouldn't produce eggs on its own. Fortunately, three of her sisters took turns coming to her house to care for Lynn and her children while she remained on bed rest for several days after the embryos were implanted.

A week after the embryo implantation, Cheryl and Hank learned that one embryo was viable. Lynn was pregnant with their child! Together with Lynn on a conference call, the thrilled couple phoned their parents and each of their siblings to share their exciting news. Within three months, Cheryl and Hank sold their home and cabin on the east coast, and moved back to Minnesota so they could help Lynn and be near Cheryl's family.

As promised, Lynn's mother and sisters rallied to help her during the pregnancy. Cheryl accompanied Lynn to every prenatal appointment. She and Hank wept with joy when they heard the sound of their baby's heart beat at the first ultrasound test. The other sisters coordinated their efforts to care for Lynn's children and help with the housework around Lynn's house, and were available by phone whenever Lynn needed support.

The pregnancy was hard on Lynn. By the third trimester, she was sick of taking shots and physically worn out. She felt like she wasn't being a good mom and eventually "hit the wall" emotionally. When Lynn felt fearful, anxious or crabby, her mood affected everyone around her. Yet despite these struggles, she knew what she was going through was worth it. She trusted that everything ultimately would be fine.

For the last month of her pregnancy, Lynn's sisters and mother took turns staying with her every night. One week before her due date, her doctor decided Lynn should be induced because she had gestational diabetes. Unfortunately, despite the doctor's attempt to "break her water," this painful procedure didn't work. Tests were done and showed the baby was "a very small, petite girl" and "not ready to come out yet." Everyone was disappointed when it was determined that Lynn, who was exhausted, had to return home and get some rest.

Several days later, Lynn returned to the hospital. With one sister (her son's godmother) caring for Lynn's children, and another one acting as a birth coach, Lynn was surrounded by the love and support of eight family members, including Cheryl and Hank, in the delivery room. This time, the inducement worked. Thanks to an epidural treatment, Lynn felt surprisingly calm and peaceful during the delivery. As soon as a perfectly healthy and beautiful little girl, "Cassie," was born, she was handed to Cheryl. The room was filled with tears of joy and happiness. According to Lynn, it was "like a party down there" until she finally asked to be alone.

Lynn knows with certainty she was the right person to carry her sister's child. Feeling blessed to have two healthy children of her own, she had no problem separating from Cheryl and Hank's baby. The tears she shed when later seeing her niece were not of sadness, but of joy and wonder at the miracle of Cassie's conception and birth.

Lynn's children welcomed their new cousin with excitement and love. During Lynn's pregnancy, her daughter often proclaimed, "My mom's having a baby and it's my cousin." Cheryl and Lynn's daughters are now more like sisters than cousins.

Lynn believes her ability to carry Cheryl and Hank's child was "meant to be." Had she not said "Yes" to the nudges that motivated her to make the generous offer, little Cassie would not be here. Her sister and husband also had to overcome their own fears and concerns to be able to say "Yes" to Lynn's loving gesture. And finally, her sisters' and mother's willingness to say "Yes" to provide Lynn's family with whatever they needed before, during, and after the pregnancy and delivery, was invaluable. Not only was it helpful to Lynn, but it allowed the rest of the family to play a part in this circle of blessing. Lynn's decision transformed Cheryl and Hank's lives as well as her own, and those of her entire family. Her story demonstrates the power of saying, "Yes" to opportunities to both give and receive gifts of kindness and love.

———————

THROUGH MEANT-TO-BE MOMENTS, WE ARE INVITED TO BE channels of love, wisdom, and faith to others and to ourselves. When we respond to opportunities to serve others, our lives take on greater meaning. In helping others in their times of need, we help ourselves to discover our greater purpose. The more we respond, the more opportunities present themselves. The result is a vibrant dialogue with the Divine and an increase in the frequency of meant-to-be experiences.

Up until now, each meant-to-be story in this book has been told separately, each illustrating one or more steps of the Living Fully process. But meant-to-be experiences can, in fact, share qualities of each step of the Living Fully process, and thus may not occur in tidy sequence. The concluding chapter tells a story that demonstrates how meant-to-be moments can accumulate over time, criss-crossing from one point in our journey to another, to create a roadmap for a fulfilling life. That story is my own.

Meant to Live Fully

The glory of God is man fully alive.

—St. Irenaeus

During the many years it took to complete this book, I've given numerous presentations, workshops, and retreats about thin places, and finding meaning within meant-to-be experiences. As previously noted, audience members and readers of my first book shared with me many of the anecdotes included here. Over time, when I told people I was writing a book about meant-to-be moments, many people expressed a similar belief to mine: that at least some of the events in our lives do seem meant to be. Other people challenged me, however, to explain how tragic and evil events could possibly have happened for any particular reason. I could not answer that question then, nor can I now.

To me, the "meant-to-be" dilemma is not an "all or nothing" one. Once I accepted the reality that we can never truly know all of God's ways or exact plan for us, I became more open to the possibility that God lets us know at least some of that plan, in part, via meant-to-be moments. I invite you to be open to that possibility, too.

My belief in that possibility motivates me to pay more attention and, if appropriate, respond to events that seem meant to be. I'm far from perfect with this process. I often resist doing what I feel "called" to do.

Yet paying attention, reflecting, asking for help, and saying "Yes" to meant-to-be moments has become the primary roadmap for how I live. Following the Living Fully process enables me to find meaning within various aspects of my life, including tragic events. It motivated me to leave a well-paying corporate position, obtain a graduate degree in theology, and eventually open a nonprofit wellness center. I've learned to trust that if God wants me to do these things, I will be given what I need to do so. And I have received everything I've *needed*, although it wasn't always what I *wanted* at the time.

Using this process is one of the most important ways I communicate with God, in addition to prayer itself. Whereas prayers are how I often talk to God, my meant-to-be moments are times when God "talks" to me. I'm not sure if prayer increases the number of these experiences in my life, but I've observed that the more I take time to talk to God, the more I notice meant-to-be moments. One of my favorite ways to pray is with Centering Prayer, a meditative process where I breathe in and breathe out while repeating sacred words in my mind. I often breathe in while mentally saying "Let Go," then breathe out while saying "Let God" or

"Let Come." Doing this for about twenty minutes once or twice daily offers all the benefits of meditation while providing a relaxing and easy way to connect with the Divine.

In this concluding chapter, I originally intended to share some of my own experiences to demonstrate how the Living Fully process works over time, through a series of meant-to-be moments. However, there are so many of these incidents, I hope to discuss them in a future book. Instead, I've included the account of how I initially became aware of the impact of meant-to-be moments.

I often am asked when I first noticed meant-to-be-moments in my own life, then I'll share the story about hearing the voice in the car, as told in the beginning of this book. But sometimes I'll add, "But I really started paying attention to them after a series of meant-to-be-moments reconnected me to an old friend shortly before he died in 1994." The story itself is too long to share in a brief conversation. I conclude this book by sharing that story here, because it demonstrates what I learned from my friend Tom about living fully.

Reconnecting with him at the end of his life taught me about the importance of paying attention and responding to a series of meant-to-be incidents. Doing so opened the door to opportunities for tremendous personal and professional growth. I developed alertness and awareness of possibilities I hadn't previously considered seriously. Because I listened to that "still, small voice," paid attention, and eventually responded to several other meant-to-be opportunities, one of those possibilities became a reality. Thanks to the dedication and support of many others, including co-founder Pat Walsh, board members, volunteers, donors, and my family and friends—who also responded to these opportunities—Well Within, the nonprofit holistic health center, opened in 2004. Over the past ten years, the center has welcomed over 23,000 visitors living with serious illnesses. When Well Within opened, I did not know about the four-part Living Fully process. I just lived it, as I continue to do now.

Meant to Be…a Friend

"I didn't find my friends; the good God gave them to me."

—Ralph Waldo Emerson

"Tom is very ill. Call him," an inner Voice directed me. Despite having a brother-in-law and several friends named "Tom," I knew immediately who this "Tom" was: my former employer and mentor. I hadn't seen Tom in nearly three years, yet I had no doubt the message spoke about him. My sense of certainty should have been a tip-off that this voice came from another source, that it spoke the truth. But it would be several months before the truth would be confirmed, several months until I could no longer ignore the signs. However, once I finally started paying attention and responding to them, I began a spiritual journey that has transformed my life.

I mentally argued with the Voice, "No, he's not sick. He's too young [mid-forties at that time]. Besides," I continued my inner rationalization, "he's always taken good care of himself. He can't be sick." In my mind, the vague shape of an obituary notice then appeared. *Was it his?* No. It couldn't be. Like a petulant child defiantly refusing to obey a parent, I ignored the command.

Tom was one of many people who have come into my life for various reasons. As a boss and mentor, he helped me develop confidence in my ability to manage a small business. As a friend, he supported my desire to balance motherhood with a career I loved. But it was his response to a life-threating disease that taught me how to live fully with a serious illness.

I first met Tom in early 1982, a few months before my second son was born. Tom managed and eventually became co-owner of a large Minneapolis travel agency. I ran a division of the agency and reported to him. We worked together for nearly five years and became good friends.

Tom was professional, competent, and had a great sense of humor. We enjoyed each other, often sharing family stories, swapping travel ideas, and comparing notes about books or movies. On a professional level, as my boss, Tom served more as a mentor than a taskmaster. As a young woman in the workplace, I appreciated the fair and respectful way he treated me. On a personal level, as a married woman, I was grateful for a friendship with a married man who was equally devoted to his young family—a friendship that was appropriate and wholesome, based on shared values and humor.

When I left the agency in 1986, I had an uneasy feeling that Tom would need my friendship some day in the future. I wrote him a note, concluding with something to this effect: "I want you to know that I have really enjoyed working with you. We probably won't see each other much from now on, but you should know that if you ever need a friend, you can count on me, even if it's years from now."

In the years that followed, Tom and I kept in touch, but only sporadically, through occasional phone calls, and a few lunches. After a Christmas lunch in 1991, I thought of him from time to time, but had not seen him again.

By autumn of 1993, my occasional thoughts of Tom took a decidedly negative turn and I heard the first directive to call him. The simple message was repeated two or three times over the next few months. I suppressed these disturbing thoughts, still not wanting to believe they might be true. Then, in late April, 1994, I happened to be visiting with an old friend from my travel industry days. She said she had heard Tom was quite ill, possibly with some form of cancer. Remembering my earlier thoughts, a cold chill shot through me. This time I paid attention to the coincidence of hearing news that affirmed the inner messages I'd received.

I was uncertain about how to respond to this information. I asked my husband for advice. Dan was surprised at my hesitation and immediately said, "Call him and offer your support!" Although I wanted to help Tom, I was still confused about what to do.

That night I could not sleep. I remembered the note I'd written to Tom years before, and felt guilty about ignoring the recent warnings of his illness. I intuitively felt I had some as yet undefined role to play in the crisis he was facing. But a conflicting negative voice said I should not meddle, my life was too hectic as it was. Tom had his family and current friends; we had not spoken in years. I didn't have the time or energy to get involved. I was a jumble of mixed emotions.

At this time in my life, prayer was not something I engaged in routinely. As a family, we said grace before meals, and perhaps a short prayer before bedtime, if one of us remembered. Prayer was not a natural first response for me, only something used when there seemed no other options were available. Now, because I was so uncertain of how to respond to the news about Tom, I prayed, asking for guidance.

At about 3 a.m., unable to sleep and in an attempt to burn off my nervous energy, I decided to clean out my long-neglected cubbyhole "office," a small closet adjoining our kitchen. While sifting through mounds of paper, I came across a page from a recent issue of *Family Circle* magazine. I did not remember having seen it before, and could not think why I would have saved it. It contained no recipes or diet ideas and no quotable words of wisdom to tape on the refrigerator door. As I was about to discard it, my eyes were drawn to a short article, in a small squared off area of the page. The article told of a woman with leukemia (I did not yet know that Tom's disease also was leukemia), whose family and friends, inspired by the book *Where Buffaloes Roam*, had showered her with love and prayers, providing her with essential support as she confronted and eventually overcame her disease. The article emphasized the importance of extending friendship to people who are ill.

Finding this article on that gloomy night was a meant-to-be moment for me; it provided the answer to my request for guidance. I understood that Tom needed my friendship, as I had foreseen intuitively many years earlier. This fortuitous incident was just what I needed on that otherwise depressing night. My agitation vanished, and I was able to go back to bed and sleep.

What followed was an emotional roller coaster that lasted nearly seven months. I called Tom the next morning. He expressed surprise at the timing of my call; he had been thinking about me, having just driven by the restaurant where we had our last lunch. After some small talk, I inquired about his health. He told me he had been diagnosed with chronic myelogenous leukemia some months earlier, shortly before my premonitions began.

Tom put a positive face on his situation. He was confident about his chances to overcome the disease. He believed that positive thinking and willpower would prevail. "You know me," he said. "I'm reading everything I can about this disease, to try and get well. One of my favorite books," he said, "is *Love, Medicine, and Miracles* by Dr. Bernie Siegel. You should read it, Mary, you'd like it too." Many years later, long after I took Tom's advice and read Siegel's excellent book, I realized doing so was my first exposure to the concept of the integration of mind, body, and spiritual healing which has since had a profound influence upon my own life.

Tom also explained that his illness had caused him to become much closer to his loved ones, especially his wife and three children. He told me: "I wouldn't wish this on anyone, but I must tell you, it's been a truly wonderful experience for me." When I asked what he meant by that surprising statement, he said he had never felt closer to his family and friends. Tom sounded so positive and optimistic that I was greatly encouraged about his chances to overcome the disease.

We ended our phone conversation with Tom saying, "I believe it's my turn to buy lunch. Let's get together. I'll call you next week." I asked if I could do anything for him before then. "Yes, you can. Pray for me." I hung up the phone, put my head in my hands, and cried.

I took seriously Tom's request for prayer. He had rarely asked any favors from me in the past twelve years, except to be more prompt at work (which I failed at miserably) and to pick him up once after he dropped his car at a service station (I was five minutes late then, too). This time, I did not want to let him down. I prayed for Tom's recovery, but I also asked that he and his family would have the strength and courage to face whatever the future held, good or bad.

We weren't able to get together for lunch for a couple of weeks. In the meantime, I attended my annual weekend silent retreat, a glorious opportunity each year to break away from my hectic day-to-day existence and reflect on where I am in my life and where I want to go.

On my retreat that year, my thoughts frequently turned to Tom. I reflected on the coincidental timing of my retreat, coming immediately before our scheduled lunch. I realized that a retreat experience could be invaluable to Tom at this critical juncture in his life, and I resolved to plant a seed and see what happened.

We met for lunch the next week as planned. Tom looked good; his illness was not physically evident. We caught up on each other's lives including our jobs and families. We then turned to his illness. The next week Tom would learn the results of an experimental treatment program he was on, which, if successful, could delay, or possibly avoid entirely, a risky bone marrow transplant procedure. He encouraged me to call him the next week, but asked that I do so near the end of the week, after he had a couple of days to digest the test results.

Toward the end of lunch, I told him about my retreat the prior weekend, and gently suggested he consider one himself. His response was noncommittal, so I did not push the issue.

Two days later, I ran into Tom while shopping at the Mall of America. We both commented on the coincidence of seeing each other twice in two days, after going nearly three years without any contact. I interpreted this synchronistic meeting as a further sign that I should be Tom's friend in the difficult times that lay ahead. I sent him his annual birthday card later that week, then waited to call him about the test results the following week.

A few days later, I experienced an overwhelming and disturbing sensation that Tom had heard bad news. This premonition was upsetting, not only because of its possible significance to Tom, but also because of its emotional impact on me. Once more, I began hearing a negative inner voice; I felt angry, in an irrational sort of way, that I was being drawn into an emotionally draining situation concerning someone whom I cared about, but who had not been a significant part of my life for many years. I then heard a different voice in my head admonish me, "Where's your faith, girl?" Immediately, the anger dissipated and I felt at peace.

I was unable to reach Tom for a couple of weeks. He was taking some time off work, which I took as confirmation that the news was not good. Then one evening, while grocery shopping, yet another overwhelming sensation occurred. It related to Tom, but the meaning was not clear. I had a strong sense that he was somehow with me, and I expected to run into him at the store, but I did not see him.

The next morning, prompted by the coincidence of reading articles about Tom's disease in both of the local newspapers, I called him again. It was his first day back at the office, and he told me he was just about to return my call. Tom confirmed the test results had been unfavorable, and confessed he was depressed at the news.

He then informed me of an odd experience he had had the evening before, about the same time I was grocery shopping. He and Joan had driven by a retreat center in a local suburb, which had prompted him to recall my suggestion at lunch a few weeks earlier. He asked me for more information, and I told him about a wonderful retreat facility for men, one that my husband visits every year. I encouraged him, saying that if nothing else, he would have three days of peace and silence, in a beautiful setting, away from everyone else's opinions and advice, and alone with his thoughts and prayers. Later, when I told Dan about my conversation with Tom, he offered to call Tom and answer any questions he might have about the retreat experience. Eventually, we both realized it would probably be best to let Tom decide without too much input from us.

I did not speak to Tom for several weeks, knowing he was preoccupied with his children's weddings. But I continued to pray for him daily, including a prayer that he would follow up on the retreat idea. I was certain it would be good for him. I wondered if I should prod him further in that direction.

One Friday morning, responding to an impulse, I called the retreat facility to see if he had ever signed up. The receptionist checked her records and, to my surprise, informed me: "He's here right now. He checked in last evening for the weekend." Amazed, I reflected on the growing list of coincidences, premonitions, intuitive nudges, and other inner messages over the past months, all of which seemed somehow destined to place Tom at the retreat facility that very weekend. I prayed for him often during the weekend: "Please, God, let him hear what you want him to hear."

Tom and I traded messages over the next couple of weeks. I learned from a former co-worker, the receptionist at his travel agency, that he had decided to proceed with the bone marrow transplant procedure and would not be working much until that treatment was completed. We were both on family vacations and did not connect by phone until the last week of August. When we finally did connect, Tom spoke at length about the weddings of his two older children, calling them "two of the happiest and most beautiful days in my life." He seemed in good spirits. He confirmed that he was going forward with the transplant procedure and was leaving his position at the travel agency. Tom expressed his gratitude to me for suggesting the retreat. The experience had been a profoundly spiritual one for him. The three days of quiet reflection and prayer in a safe, structured environment had helped him come to grips with and accept his predicament. After talking for about an hour, we decided to continue our conversation over lunch the next week.

When we met that day, what struck me most was how much he seemed to have grown as a person. Tom had always been a great guy, but there had been a certain reserve about him. Despite his outgoing personality, people could only get so close to him. Now he seemed more open. He was willing, even anxious, to talk at a deeper, more personal level. For the first time, we discussed our faith and other spiritual issues. Tom spoke with enthusiasm about his recent retreat experience, regretting he had not started this tradition years earlier. He had read some books about living more fully and had absorbed this basic message: Each day, every moment, is a gift, an opportunity for joy that should not be squandered. Tom quite clearly had reached a deeper spiritual level in his life. The combination of his positive attitude plus his deepening spirituality helped him find peace and the strength to deal with adversity.

Tom spoke of how his illness had changed his priorities. He yearned for a simpler life than the hectic existence he'd lived as a corporate executive. He had decided to change careers after his transplant. "I would like to be a counselor," he confided, "and work with other people who are dealing with life-threatening illnesses. Maybe I can help them."

His priorities, it seemed, now were on relationships—with God, with his family, with his friends—not on material possessions, or the worries and distractions of his prior executive lifestyle.

In one way, this lunch was a terribly sad one, yet I did not cry. Tom was peaceful. He was having fun, golfing with his sons and friends, and planning a getaway that weekend with his wife at a charming and romantic bed-and-breakfast establishment in a nearby river town. He was secure in his faith and with himself. He was not bitter or despondent. His parting comment to me was most reassuring: "I feel I am really ready for this, no matter what happens."

As we parted that day, he thanked me again for my support and friendship, and he confirmed how helpful it was to have people he could talk to about what he was going through. We hugged—something else he would never have done in years past—and agreed we would get together again after his hospital stay. I did not, could not, say good-bye to him.

After Tom entered the hospital, I was uncertain about my continuing role. Tom's family did not know me and I did not want to get in the way. Tom's sister-in-law, Barb, put together a mailing list of his friends and relatives, and she was kind enough to add me to the list. I was encouraged by the willingness of Tom's family to include me within the circle of his caring friends. Tom and I spoke by phone a couple of times over the next few days. He thanked me for some Johnny Carson *Tonight Show* videos I had sent him.

When I called a few days later, Tom already had received the bone marrow from his sister. He sounded weak and groggy, and we did not talk long. Another mailing from Tom's family arrived at about the same time, discussing the transplant. The letter was hopeful and upbeat. It told of a kind gesture by Gary Player, the famous golfer, who was a spokesperson for Tom's wife, Joan's, company. Mr. Player had called to wish Tom well. Tom responded with his typical humor, noting that because he had received his sister's bone marrow, he intended, in the future, to demand the right to hit from the shorter ladies' tees. The letter also explained that the first twenty-one days after the transplant were crucial, and asked for everyone's prayers. It ended with a message from Tom, wishing God's blessing from the "Impatient Patient" to all his friends and relatives who were so supportive.

Three weeks after the transplant, near the end of the crucial twenty-one-day period, I dropped off a small congratulatory gift and card to be delivered to Tom's room. That afternoon I received a call from Barb. Tom suddenly had stopped breathing earlier that day. He had been revived and his doctors had induced a coma-like condition to allow Tom to rest so his body could heal. In the days that followed, I continued to pray for Tom and his family, but I also sadly faced the fact that he might die. A few days later, I called the hospital for an update. Joan's mother answered the phone in his room. "It doesn't look good," she said. Later that day, Barb called, with sad news. Around 4 p.m., surrounded by his family and the music of his favorite hymn, "Amazing Grace," Tom had died.

Three days later, I was getting dressed to attend the funeral that so many had prayed would not occur. The past few days had been filled with tears, but there was also an element of joy in the belief that my friend now was at peace and reaping his heavenly reward, free of the pain he had endured, with such dignity, during the past few weeks. And while there is always tragedy associated with the death of a friend or loved one, especially in the prime of life, I was comforted that Tom had well-prepared himself to meet his fate.

As I dressed, I vacillated between two different colored jackets to wear over my simple black dress. A traditional black jacket, signifying the somber grief that accompanies death, was deemed most appropriate at first. Then, I saw my favorite one, its blood-red color symbolically affirming Tom's new eternal life. The color of mourning reigned, just for an instant. Reaching for the black jacket, once again, I heard the voice that had guided me through my friend's illness. I smiled as I listened to the consoling message: "Wear the red one." This time I obeyed it.

Tom died despite the countless prayers of family and friends for his survival. I had interpreted the many coincidences and intuitive nudges as signs that God intended for Tom to live. When the voice asked, "Where's your faith?" I assumed it meant my friend would be miraculously cured. But this was not to be.

In his final days, Tom was surrounded by people who were channels of God's love during the most difficult time in his life. Before he was hospitalized, Tom's golfing buddies kept him physically active with his favorite sport. During the bone marrow transplant process, co-workers, fellow travel industry professionals, and many others helped set a hospital record for cards and letters received by a patient.

Among his family and close friends who showered him with affection, one special man even shaved his own head just to hear a hearty laugh from his pain-wracked friend. Those who rallied to Tom's side responded to a call, we thought, to help him live. Instead, without knowing it at the time, we were asked to help him prepare to die.

I know now that the question about my faith directed me toward a choice: to trust that all would be well, whether Tom lived or died. I believe that he is just fine, welcomed into a wondrous new eternal life by the God who never abandoned him. My faith tells me that.

But the experience with my friend also left me with a desire to explore several questions about the incidents I observed. *What is the role of the inner voices we hear? How can coincidences help us live a fuller life? How can we find meaning in tragic events? Where is God in the midst of grief? Does prayer really help?* To learn more, I had to set aside any inhibitions about speaking about my own spiritual experiences. I had to become comfortable discussing "God." I had to choose to not only honor, but also learn from the stories of people with vastly different religious beliefs from mine.

Upon reflection, I realized that Tom, and later his wife, Joan, helped me see that God does not abandon us in our darkest hours. If we search for it, it's possible to find the good that can come from tragic experiences. God is there to comfort us, to give us strength, to provide us with guidance and direction. And in the midst of tragic events, God creates opportunities for growth, and for grace.

God's presence in my friend's situation could be seen in innumerable ways. For Tom, his time of sickness also was a time of personal and spiritual growth. As he approached his death, he lived more fully than ever. Living fully in the present moment, he nurtured and cherished his relationships with God, his family, and his friends. He was positive and appreciative of the many small joys in daily life. He was at peace. Keenly aware of the concern his tragic situation prompted, Tom had assured his loved ones that he had achieved a sense of peace. He often expressed his belief that "there must be a reason for my illness." When he first said this to me, I wanted to argue with him and ask, "What possible reason could there be for someone to suffer from a terminal illness?"

The reality is that none of us really knows why things do, or don't, happen. But for Tom, believing his illness "happened for a reason" caused him to find meaning within his situation. He did this in two ways. First, by being grateful for the positive aspects of a life-threatening illness. For example, he expressed gratitude for the opportunity that his sickness gave him to prepare for his death. He once told me, "No one knows when his or her time is up. A car could hit you or me this afternoon. This way, I can prepare myself and my family for whatever the future may bring." Second, he found meaning in his determination to use his experience to help others. Even though he didn't get to fulfill his dream of becoming a counselor, Tom shared what he learned so others could benefit from the wisdom that so often comes with life's biggest challenges and struggles.

Tom's family also experienced God's presence and grace. This is not meant to suggest that Tom's death somehow was a positive experience for his family. For Joan, the loss of her husband left "an empty hole in my heart that will remain there forever." But Joan also told me how much closer she has grown to her children as a result of Tom's illness and death. Her words carry meaning for all of us: "Mary, be grateful for your family, especially your children. You never know what lies ahead. Since Tom's death, I tell my children at every opportunity how much I love them." Joan's strong faith and God's grace were a great comfort for both her and Tom during his illness, and later in coming to grips with Tom's death. Grief can bring us closer to God if we allow ourselves to be open to God's love and support during the most difficult times in our lives.

The experience of reconnecting with Tom during the final months of *his* life transformed *my* life. I still don't know if there was a "reason" he became terminally ill. But I'm so grateful for the opportunity to observe how this belief influenced his response to his situation. Tom taught me that being open to the possibility that some things are "meant to be" brings us comfort, provides hope, and nudges us to take advantage of the opportunities in our lives to grow and become the person we are meant to be by the God who created us. Saying "Yes" to the meant-to-be nudges that prompted me to reach out to him was the first step of a midlife journey that eventually motivated me to leave the corporate world and do what Tom had wanted to do: Counsel people living with life-threatening illnesses.

Bibliography and Resources

Borg, Marcus, *The Heart of Christianity: Rediscovering a Life of Faith*. New York: HarperOne, 2004.

Bonhoeffer, Dietrich. *Letters and Papers from Prison*. Minneapolis: Fortress Press, 2010.

Borysenko, Joan, PhD. Interview with Mary Treacy O'Keefe on Hope, Healing and WellBeing radio show: "From Fried to Revived." Webtalkradio.net. (http://tinyurl.com/qcbyjdw)

Buber, Martin, and Ronald Gregor Smith. *I and Thou*. Reprint, Edinburgh: T. & T. Clark, 2011.

Buechner, Frederick. *Listening to Your Life: Daily Meditations with Frederick Buechner*. New York: HarperOne, 1992.

Frankl, Victor. *Man's Search for Meaning*. Boston: Beacon Press, 2006.

Gallup, George H., Jr. "Americans Feel Need to Believe." *Gallup.com*, January 15, 2002.

Guenther, Margaret. *Holy Listening: The Art of Spiritual Direction*. London: Darton, Longman & Todd, 1993.

Hilton, Conrad. *Be My Guest*. New York: Fireside, 1984.

Holy Bible, New American Standard Version. La Habra, California: The Lockman Foundation, 2013.

Holy Bible, New International Version, Grand Rapids, MI: Zondervan, 2012.

Holy Bible, King James Version. Oxford, England: Oxford University Press, 2008.

http://www.ignatianspirituality.com/ignatian-prayer/the-examen.

James, William, *Varieties of Religious Experiences*, New York: St. Martin's, 2012.

Job, Rueben, *A Guide to Spiritual Discernment*. Nashville: Upper Room Books, 1996.

Jung, Carl. *Synchronicity: An Acausal Connecting Principle*. (From Vol. 8. of the Collected Works of C. G. Jung). Princeton, NJ: Princeton University Press, 2012.

Lewis, C. S. *Mere Christianity*. Fiftieth anniversary ed. London: HarperCollins, 2002.

Linn, Dennis, Linn, Matthew, S.J. and Sheila Fabricant Linn. *Sleeping with Bread: Holding What Gives You Life*. Mahwah, N.J.: Paulist Press, 1995.

Martin, James, S.J.. *The Jesuit Guide to (Almost) Everything: A Spirituality for Real Life*. San Francisico, CA: HarperOne, 2012.

Mooty, Raymond. *Life After Life: The Investigation of a Phenomenon-Survival of Bodily Death*. New York: HarperOne, 1975.

Morris, Danny E., and Charles M. Olsen. *Discerning God's Will Together: Aspirational Practice for the Church*. Downer's Grove, IL: Intervarsity Press, 2012.

O'Donohue, John. *Anam Cara*. New York: Harper Perennial, 2009.

Parker Pope, Tara. "What Are Friends For? A Longer Life." *New York Times*, April 21, 2009.

Parker Pope, Tara. "Most Believe God Gets Involved." *New York Times*, March 10, 2010.

Rilke, Rainer Maria. *Letters to a Young Poet*. New York: W.W. Norton, 1993.

Scott Schieman. 2010. "Socioeconomic Status and Beliefs about God's Influence in Everyday Life," *Sociology of Religion*, 71:1: 25-51.

Sellner, Edward C. *Mentoring: The Ministering of Spiritual Kinship*. Cambridge, MA: Cowley, 2002.

Shannon, Maggie Oman. *PRAYERS FOR HEALING: 365 Blessings, Poems, and Meditations From Around The World*. Newburyport, MA: Conari Press, 2000.

Teasdale, Wayne. *The Mystic Heart: Discovering a Universal Spirituality in the World's Religions*. Novato, CA: New World Library, 2001.

Vest, Norvene. *No Moment Too Small: Rhythms of Silence, Prayer and Holy Reading*. Lanham, MD: Cowley, 2004.

Author Information

Note: many of the authors of the Meant-to-Be stories chose to remain anonymous or asked to use just their first name. Below is information from authors who permitted this information to be included in this book:

Glenna Belland:

Glenna is a Healing Touch Certified Practitioner through the Healing Touch Program and a graduate of the Christos Center for Spiritual Formation as spiritual director. She is a facilitator and teacher of prayer forms and relationship with God and retreat leader. Glenna also is a teammate with Listening Points Ministry, lpministry.com.

Dorienne:

Dorienne's website is: africanstay.co.za.

Mary Ferguson:

Since sharing her story in *Meant-to-Be Moments*, Mary writes that Rick migrated to the United States and both of them are now living in Indianapolis with Mary's adult daughter. Rick loves living in the U.S.

Doris Fortino:

Doris Fortino lives in Italy and leads tours of the country. She is the owner of Ancora Italia, a real estate rental service in Tuscany. Her website is ancoraitalia.com.

Nora Giglio:

Nora loves sewing, crocheting and designing homemade crafts. She's been married to Joe for thirty-three years, has three children, and is the very happy and proud grandma to her first granddaughter, Alexandra Rose. Her website is miabaggali.com.

Becky Henry:

Hope Network, LLC Founder and national award-winning author Becky Henry is a mom on a mission, using her professional life coaching training to educate about eating disorders and guide parents through the recovery process. Her website is eatingdisorderfamilysupport.com

Cheryl Hiltibran:

Cheryl's website is goinggenius.com.

Carmela Tursi Hobbins:

Carmela Tursi Hobbins has written two cookbooks, *Carmela's Cucina* and *Celebrations With Carmela's Cucina*. She is a culinary instructor and hosts culinary and cultural tours to Italy. Her website is carmiescucina.com.

Marlene King, MA

Marlene is a writer, artist, dream consultant, mental health professional, and former corporate executive. Her long-standing column, *Dream Times*, appears in *Dream Network Journal* and she utilizes the expressive arts and Jungian perspectives to guide her clients to explore the meaning of their dreams. She resides in the Pacific Northwest with her husband, cockatoo, and two cats. To contact Marlene, please visit dreamtimesguide.com or email her at marlene@dreamtimesguide.com.

Dave Norby:

Dave has spent his career in the consumer food industry. He makes his home with his wife Joni in the Central Valley of California. Dave's hobbies include farming and traveling back and forth to Minnesota to visit their daughter, Katie.

Leela Ugargol

At the age of sixteen, Leela Ugargol came to United States from her native India. She credits her parents with enriching her own spirituality. The bond continued and grew stronger after her father's death and changed Leela's life direction. She now teaches Reiki classes, works with past lives, does soul connections, and gives energy treatments. Contact her at reikibypinklotus@gmail.com.

Tom (story in chapter 6):

Tom's websites are xenakisarts.com and xenakisiconarts. com.

Theresa Zimanske:

Theresa Zimanske is a Minnesota mother dramatically changed by her son Michael's rare syndrome. She shares personal experiences about God's faithfulness, letting go, and discovering what God created her to be after the death of her son.

Acknowledgments

I AM GRATEFUL TO THE MANY PEOPLE WHO HELPED WITH the creation of this book. Thank you to everyone who has ever shared a meant-to-be experience with me, including at my presentations, in touching letters and emails, and during fascinating conversations. Special thanks to those who have graciously allowed me to share their stories here. Many of you contributed anonymously. To all of you and anyone else who provided assistance, information, and inspiration, please feel deeply appreciated, even if your name is not listed here.

To Joan Truso and her late husband Tom, for enabling me to understand the importance of paying attention and responding to meant-to-be moments.

To Michelle Hogdson, my wise and gifted primary editor, for her professional expertise and persistent encouragement during the many years it took to finish this book.

To Diane Keyes, Sherri Hildebrandt, and Laura Zats for additional editorial and proofreading assistance.

To Lisa Hagan, Laurie Harper, and Jan B. King for their literary advice and professional assistance.

To the wonderful Women of Words (WOW), including co-founders Connie Anderson and Colleen Szot, for their invaluable support, encouragement and treasured friendship.

To the dedicated staff, board, volunteers, supporters, and participants of Well Within, a source of inspiration, support and hope for people living with serious illnesses.

To the generous individuals who read all or part of *Meant-to-Be Moments* and provided invaluable feedback: Connie Anderson, Jill DeLisi, Bernadette Dodge, Dr. Henry Emmons, Ellen Glatstein, Becky Henry, Dr. Mary Jo Kreitzer, Fr. John Malone, Dr. Bill Manahan, Pamela Muldoon, Dr. Eldon Taylor, Fr. Paul Treacy, Dr. Jean Wiger.

To Fr. John Malone with gratitude for his wise spiritual guidance and delightful wit.

To Rabbi Harold Kushner for sharing his profound wisdom and helping me clarify my thoughts regarding whether things happen for a reason.

To my Treacy siblings, O'Keefe in-laws and their families for their priceless support, love, and friendship.

To the soul friends who have listened to my meant-to-be moments, shared their own stories, and blessed my life for more than twenty years: Jan Berens, Holly Cashin, Debbie Donnelly, Mary Gale, Ellen Glatstein, Maureen Grau, Terry Noel, and Barb Semerad.

To the Wise Ink team, Dara Moore Beevas, Amy Quale, Laura Zats, and Amara Thein for their creative suggestions and professional expertise.

To Ryan Scheife at Mayfly Design for designing the interior and cover of this book.

To my beloved children, Peter, Bill, Emily, and Tim, wonderful daughter-in-laws Renee and Meghan and future son-in-law Sol, and the grandchildren that soon will grace our lives.

Finally, to my husband Dan whose support, encouragement, and enduring love has enabled me to live life to the fullest every day.

A Note from the Author

THANK YOU FOR READING MEANT-TO-BE MOMENTS! I HOPE that doing so reminded you of some of your past spiritual experiences and motivates you to pay attention to future ones. If you would like to share a significant meant-to-be story, it might be used in an upcoming book. Please email your stories or comments regarding this book to mtbstories@gmail.com or mail them to:

Mary Treacy O'Keefe
P.O. Box 18492
St. Paul, MN 55118

To contact me about possible speaking engagements or appearances, please visit marytreacyokeefe.com or send an email to mary.treacy.okeefe@gmail.com.

Net proceeds from the sale of *Meant-to-Be Moments* will support the integrative healing services at Well Within and other charitable organizations. For more information or to make a donation to Well Within, please visit wellwithin.org.

About Mary Treacy O'Keefe

Mary Treacy O'Keefe is the author of *Thin Places: Where Faith is Affirmed and Hope Dwells*. She is co-founder of Well Within (wellwithin.org), a nonprofit holistic wellness center that provides low-cost or free integrative healing services, support, classes, and therapies to people living with serious illnesses and other challenges. A certified spiritual director with a master's degree in Theology, she also is host of the Hope, Healing and WellBeing internet radio show. She has four grown children and lives with her husband a few miles from her hometown of St. Paul, Minnesota. For more information, please visit marytreacyokeefe.com